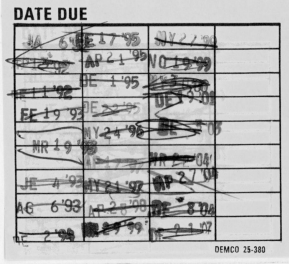

Sylvia Plath

Sylvia Plath _____

The Poetry of Initiation

by Jon Rosenblatt

THE UNIVERSITY OF NORTH CAROLINA PRESS
CHAPEL HILL

Acknowledgments

John Berryman: from *The Dream Songs*. Copyright © 1959, 1962, 1963, 1964, 1965, 1966, 1967, 1968, 1969. Reprinted by permission of Farrar, Straus & Giroux, Inc., and Faber and Faber Ltd.

Robert Lowell: from *Life Studies*. Copyright © 1956, 1959. Reprinted by permission of Farrar, Straus & Giroux, Inc., and Faber and Faber Ltd.

Robin Morgan: from *Monster: Poems*. Copyright © 1961, 1962, 1963, 1965, 1966, 1967, 1968, 1970, 1971, 1972. Reprinted by permission of Random House, Inc./Alfred A. Knopf, Inc.

Sylvia Plath: *Ariel*. Copyright © 1965 by Ted Hughes. Reprinted by permission of Harper & Row, Publishers, Inc. Published in Great Britain by Faber and Faber Ltd. Reprinted by permission of Olwyn Hughes;
from *The Colossus and Other Poems*. Copyright © 1957, 1958, 1959, 1960, 1961, 1962. Reprinted by permission of Random House, Inc./Alfred A. Knopf, Inc. Published in Great Britain by Faber and Faber Ltd. Reprinted by permission of Olwyn Hughes;
"The Couriers." Copyright © 1963 by Ted Hughes; "Words." Copyright © 1965 by Ted Hughes; portions of "Totem," "Death & Co.," "Elm," "Poppies in October," and "Fever 103°." Copyright © 1965 by Ted Hughes. All from *Ariel*. Copyright © 1965 by Ted Hughes. Reprinted by permission of Harper & Row, Publishers, Inc. Published in Great Britain by Faber and Faber Ltd. Reprinted by permission of Olwyn Hughes;
from *Crossing the Water*. Copyright © 1971 by Ted Hughes. Reprinted by permission of Harper & Row, Publishers, Inc. Published in Great Britain by Faber and Faber Ltd. Reprinted by permission of Olwyn Hughes;
from *Winter Trees*. Copyright © 1971, 1972 by Ted Hughes. Reprinted by permission of Harper & Row, Publishers, Inc. Published in Great Britain by Faber and Faber Ltd. Reprinted by permission of Olwyn Hughes.

John Crowe Ransom: from *Selected Poems*, Third Edition, Revised and Enlarged. Copyright © 1969. Reprinted by permission of Random House, Inc./Alfred A. Knopf, Inc.

Theodore Roethke: from *Collected Poems*. Copyright © 1937, 1954, 1957, 1958, 1959, 1960, 1961, 1962, 1963, 1964, 1965, 1966. Reprinted by permission of Doubleday and Company.

Anne Sexton: "Sylvia's Death" and "Those Times . . ." from *Live or Die*. Copyright © 1966. Reprinted by permission of Houghton Mifflin Company and the Sterling Lord Agency.

Dylan Thomas: "I See the Boys of Summer," "The Force That Through the Green Fuse," "After the Funeral" from *The Poems of Dylan Thomas*. Copyright © 1938, 1939 by New Directions Publishing Corporation. Reprinted by permission of New Directions Publishing Corporation, J. M. Dent & Sons Ltd., Publishers (*Collected Poems of Dylan Thomas*), and the Trustees for the Copyrights of the late Dylan Thomas.

A portion of chapter 2 has been published previously in somewhat different form in *Twentieth Century Literature* (December 1978). A portion of Chapter 5 has been published previously in somewhat different form in *The Explicator* (December 1975).

© 1979 The University of North Carolina Press

1. Plath, Sylvia—Criticism and interpretation.
2. Initiations in literature. I. Title.
PS3566.L27Z87   811'.5'4   78-14023
ISBN 0-8078-1338-9

To Carol

Contents

Preface

I began this study of Sylvia Plath's poetry out of a desire to understand the relationship between two aspects of her work: its powerful images and rhythms and its ritual or quasi-ritual patterns. When I first read the poems eight or nine years ago, I thought that their imagistic and rhythmic intensity derived from a personal ritual process. I saw Plath as a poet who had attempted something essentially different from the contemporary writers with whom she was normally associated, Theodore Roethke, Robert Lowell, John Berryman, and Anne Sexton. She linked private images and motifs into sequences that formed part of a coherent drama, a symbolic enactment. This dramatic approach was the key to her last poems, mainly collected in *Ariel* and *Winter Trees*, which take the reader into a world of heightened possibilities and fatal attractions. I conceived of her work as a poetry of personal process in which the central development was an initiation, a transformation of the self from a state of symbolic death to one of rebirth. Her death in 1963 cut off the life of a poet who had only just found a method for dramatizing the warring forces of her personal universe.

Yet when I came to read the criticism that dealt with Plath's poetry, I saw that only a few writers even began to speak of the poems in the way I thought appropriate. Over the last few years the situation has improved only slightly. Virtually all of the critical commentary focuses on issues that are irrelevant to the work and to an understanding of its power. Most writers use the poems only to support their discussions of cultural and biographical problems. The cultural critics insist on seeing Plath as an "exemplary" figure of the time. The biographically oriented writers use the quotations from *Ariel* as touchstones for a commentary on the poet's victimization or heroism or psychopathology. To give one example: the enormous interest in madness and schizophrenia beginning in the 1960s has made Plath a prime subject for analysis. Her only novel, *The Bell Jar*, records her breakdown and suicide attempt; and her poems are full of hallucinated images. But from *Time* to *Literature and Psychology*, the magazines have treated Plath essentially as a famous suicide, converting her art into a document in the career of a madwoman. In books like Phyllis Chesler's *Women and Madness* and, more recently, Otto Friedrich's *Going Crazy*, Plath becomes nothing more than a case history. Her reputation as a poet provides a kind of excuse for discussion of her madness. It is not difficult to see that such an appropriation of Plath's poetry can never result in an adequate understanding or evaluation of its achievement.

Certainly there are a few good, specifically literary studies that attempt to define the kind of poetry that Plath wrote and that make first steps toward a reading of the poems, especially those published over the past two years. Ted Hughes's brief essay on *Crossing the Water* and his "Notes on the Chronological Order of Sylvia Plath's Poems" are notable for their precision and tact. Marjorie Perloff, in *The Poetic Art of Robert Lowell*, has effectively shown that the recurrent comparison between Plath and Lowell is inaccurate, although her attempt to define Plath as a poet of animism, in *"Angst* and Animism in the Poetry of Sylvia Plath," is, I think, inadequate. Elizabeth Hardwick, Joyce Carol Oates, and Linda Wagner have written sensitive general essays on the poetry. Edward Butscher's critical biography, *Sylvia Plath: Method and Madness*, includes many perceptive analyses of the poems, although his comments are nearly buried under a mass of psychoanalytic interpretations of Plath's life. Butscher has performed the invaluable service of talking to virtually everyone who was ever connected with Plath and of organizing information about the phases of her career, but his psychological understanding of her life and poetry must be taken as a largely hypothetical and unconvincing construction. The recent study of Plath's mythological sources by Judith Kroll, *Chapters in a Mythology: The Poetry of Sylvia Plath*, fills gaps in our knowledge about Plath's reading and about her manuscript revisions. Unfortunately, it also imposes an extremely misleading system on the poetry. Kroll reads all the images and symbols in the poems after 1959 as coded elements for aspects of the Great Mother myth that Robert Graves expounded in *The White Goddess*. Kroll's systematic interpretation of every color, object, and figure in the poems falsifies the character of Plath's work in two ways. First, Plath's development of key images (moon, black and white, stone, water) can be traced back to poems that antedate her reading of *The White Goddess* in 1959. One of the main points of my chapter on *The Colossus* is, in fact, that the imagistic and ideological elements in the later poetry are already present in embryonic form as early as 1955 and 1956. Plath's views of death and rebirth do not possess the simplicity and consistency of Graves's mythological system. They reflect, instead, the contradictions and self-division of lived experience.

Second, Plath's later poetry cannot be explained as "mystical" or "transcendent" poetry, even though Plath may have been familiar with mystical literature. To read her very last poems, like "Edge" and "Words," as examples of a "transcendent perspective" on death is to ignore the obvious despair and sense of failure that informs them. If Kroll's readings were to be followed, Plath would appear as a Zen Buddhist, who had reached the desired state of "no-mind." And yet what difference there is between the calm of the Buddhist monk and the neutralized blankness of Plath's very last work!

Given the tendentious and extraliterary nature of most criticism on Plath, then, it is not hard to see that almost no one reads her poems as poetry. Whether praising or damning Plath, critics see her poems through the distorting lens of biographical criticism. Thus, any reading that makes a claim to being accurate and comprehensive has to begin by showing that Plath is not the poet whom her critics either admire or denigrate. It has to prove that her poetry can be discussed as literature. The order and argument of this study follow, then, from my sense that Plath's poems do deserve consideration for their literary qualities and methods.

In my first chapter, I have set down the grounds for rejecting three major misconceptions about Plath's life and art. These misconceptions all derive from the problem of interpreting a body of personal poetry in which autobiographical material plays a considerable part. It is my general contention that such personal poetry is not an invention of American poets since World War II, but has existed for thousands of years; that it deserves the same critical attention as any other body of poetry; and that the personal origin of imagery and event in poetry neither validates nor invalidates the work. The fact that Plath makes numerous personal references in her poems is not the distinguishing characteristic of her literary art; two thousand years ago Catullus patterned his lyrics around autobiographical events to a much greater degree than Plath. The important issue in reading her poems is the consistency and depth she obtains in elaborating her themes.

Specifically, I have argued that the dominant misunderstandings of Plath's work arise because of a faulty interpretation of her biographical and literary situation. Views that emphasize Plath's feminism, her suicide, and her confessionalism appear to me to have been most damaging to a clear and balanced reading of her poems. When the inaccuracies of these interpretive schemas have been revealed, her work can no longer be seen in terms of her biography but of her desire to enact an initiatory transformation through art.

My approach in the first two chapters is necessarily structural and thematic rather than chronological because the aims and methods of Plath's work must be established before any sequential treatment of the poems can take place. Although

Plath's step-by-step development of a poetry of initiation is of great interest, the essential point is that she did finally arrive at a coherent strategy for her poetry. The dramatic plot of her later poems and her handling of image sequences are the most significant characteristics of her final year (1962–63). In Chapter 2, I have shown how these poems can be read within the dramatic and thematic context of her drive toward self-transformation. Her characteristic imagery, which is split between positive and negative poles, follows to a remarkable degree the imagery of initiatory practices. Plath's dramatic approach to the lyric form can also be understood as an outgrowth of her attempt to imitate ritual processes. Through close readings of a number of significant poems, I demonstrate in detail how plot, image, and character combine to produce Plath's particular lyric form.

Plath's discovery of the initiatory structure and of her imagistic method is the subject of Chapter 3. The sense of world and of self that inform *The Bell Jar* and the later poetry can be seen in the poems Plath wrote between 1950 and 1959. In *The Colossus*, Plath's first volume of poems, she began to organize the perceptual world through a series of polarities (hardness-softness, naturalness-artificiality) and focused upon a handful of significant images (sea, stone, father, animals). Her habit of thinking in opposites and of employing a small number of important images provided the basis for the later personal poetry in which a few personal images and tremendous psychic oppositions predominate. In the later poems of *The Colossus*, the central concerns of her initiatory imagination appear: the fear of physical harm and death; motherhood; and the poet's sense of an emerging selfhood. Out of the static and awkward poems written before 1959, Plath developed her dynamic vision of the battle between self and others and self and nature.

One of the key elements in the transition between Plath's earlier and later work is her use of landscape and seascape as both a correlative for the psychological processes described in the poems and a source of images. Chapter 4 shows that her manner of internalizing natural objects eventually permitted her to arrive at a thoroughgoing symbolic representation of psychic process. The shift from earlier to later modes of landscape poetry parallels the movement of her entire career: from traditional to open forms; from a static imagery of the external world to a dynamic imagery of the body and inner world. In studying Plath's perception and use of nature, I find that she attributed radically antithetical emotional meanings to identical natural objects and that her larger concerns with death and birth, hate and love, are mirrored in this dualistic treatment of the fundamental elements, water and land, sky and stars.

The fifth chapter turns to the powerful dramas of *Ariel* and *Winter Trees*. Here the self finds situations and dramatic forms that objectify the battle between life and death forces. In these brilliant, though sometimes chaotic poems, Plath continually dramatizes her encounter with death. Writing out of her dual obsession with annihilation and salvation, she converts the various subjects of her poetry into instances of the death-and-rebirth pattern: the love and hatred within the family; the situation of women in marriage; the relation between self and nature. I argue that in the best of these late poems Plath attains an equilibrium between the forces of her existence and that her method organizes perception and language into a powerful aesthetic whole.

My study ends with a chapter on the relationship between poetry and suffering, a relationship that darkens both Plath's work and much of our contemporary consciousness of literature. In comparing Plath with her contemporaries, it seems evident that she was working within a context of poetic endeavor that culminated in the late 1960s and early 1970s. Although I believe that Plath was specifically mapping her own poetry of initiation, there are important links between her work and that of Roethke, Lowell, Berryman, and Sexton. A heightened awareness of the individual's painful entrapment in contemporary society becomes the central focus of their poems. Plath's poetry of initiatory transformation thus appears, within its general social framework, as a means of escape from the identities and forces that imprison the self in America.

In the preparation of this book I have incurred debts to a number of teachers and friends. Ronald Moran was unfailingly supportive during the period when I conceived this study and wrote the first of its several versions. C. Hugh Holman and George Lensing read a prior manuscript and made valuable comments. Paul Zweig and Luke Meyers encouraged me in the project and suggested certain lines of argument. Financial support has been provided by Rhode Island College. My wife, Carol Simon Rosenblatt, has endured through the various stages of the book and deserves more than one dedication for her understanding and help.

Providence, R.I.   *Jon Rosenblatt*
April 1978   RHODE ISLAND COLLEGE

Sylvia Plath

one _____

Misconceptions

Your face broods from my table, Suicide. [1]
                            —John Berryman

Thief! —
how did you crawl into,

crawl down alone
into the death I wanted so badly and for so long, . . . [2]
                            —Anne Sexton

We continue to brood about Sylvia Plath in ways that have
more to do with our own obsessions than with hers. Since her
death in 1963, she has become at once a heroine of suicide, a
martyr, a madwoman, and a prophet. Because these are essen-
tially archetypal categories, it is not surprising that Plath the
writer, author of one novel and a few slim volumes of poetry,
has been lost amid a torrent of public fantasies and projections.
Only three years after the suicide, Robert Lowell offered an
extraordinary account of why Plath would never be accepted
as *merely* a writer. She was, according to Lowell, "hardly a
person at all, or a woman, certainly not another 'poetess,' but
one of those superreal, hypnotic, great classical heroines."[3]
This statement might appear to be a rhetorical exaggeration,
but the response of Plath's audience to her work over the past
ten years has borne out Lowell's description. The hypnotic
appeal of the poet-heroine has affected virtually every reader.
Even so cautious a critic as Stephen Spender could imagine
that the *Ariel* poems were "written by some priestess cultivat-

ing her hysteria, come out of Nazi and war-torn Europe, gone to America, and then situated on the rocky Cornish Atlantic coast."[4] By the end of the 1960s, Plath had been identified with Cassandra, Electra, Medea, Emily Dickinson, and Virginia Woolf. By the 1970s, she has become all things to all people. We can hardly distinguish any longer between the poetry and the tissues of fantasy, hyperbole, misreading, and misconception that have grown over it.

Yet an effort must be made to separate Plath and her poetry from the fascinating but misleading speculations of her audience. Three misconceptions of her artistic and biographical situation have gained the widest attention over the last decade and deserve detailed analysis. The first centers upon Plath's supposed victimization by a male-dominated culture and her consequent feminist or protofeminist attitudes; the second upon her suicide and its heroic or romantic aspects; and the third upon the confessional nature of her poetry and her view of art. The first two of these approaches to Plath's career involve interpretations of her biography that have major consequences for any understanding of the poetry; the confessional interpretation asserts an inescapable relationship between biography and poetry in Plath's case. All three misconceptions must be clarified before we can consider the actual aims and structures of her poems.

Certainly the dominant biographical interpretation of Plath's career over the past ten years has been feminist in orientation. Plath has appeared as a representative female victim in the literature on sexual politics, a casualty of the patriarchal world of marriage and art. Germaine Greer, for example, has claimed that Plath would not have committed suicide had she been alive during the late sixties and early seventies when the women's liberation movement developed.[5] Apparently, Greer believes that Plath's feminist awareness had not been sufficiently formed by the time of her death to allow her to resist victimization and oppression by men. Other writers have argued that Plath possessed a feminist or at least a protofeminist consciousness of sexual political issues; they support this claim by citing poems by Plath that express rage at men. Finally, feminist writers have generally agreed that Plath was actually victimized by the men around her.

The feminist use of Plath as an exemplary figure, however, is a mixture of truth and fantasy. Take, for instance, this analysis of Plath's "case" by Phyllis Chesler, a psychologist: "Plath was lonely and isolated. Her genius did not earn for her certain reprieves and comforts tendered the male artist. No one, and especially men of culture, felt 'responsible' for her plight or felt responsible to honor the poet by 'saving' the woman. After separating from her husband, Plath continued to write and keep house for her children. On the night of February 10 [sic] or the morning of February 11, 1963, she killed herself."[6] Or, here is the analysis by the feminist Robin Morgan in a poem called "Arraignment" that accuses

> A. Alvarez,
> George Steiner, Robert Lowell,
> and the legions of critical necrophiles
> of conspiracy to mourn Plath's brilliance while
> patronizing her madness, diluting her rage,
> burying her politics. . . . [7]

In these versions of feminist criticism, Plath is the classic victim of male neglect, male contempt for women, and male chauvinist discrimination. Her death is a form of martyrdom; her life, a case history in the devilish cultural politics that favor men over women and destroy women's creativity.

The general feminist indictment of masculine attitudes toward women in the arts and the cultural life contains a good deal of truth, but the specific statements about Plath's biography are untrue. A close look at Plath's biography indicates that the line of argument pursued by Chesler and others involves misinterpretation and distortion. Plath's career was extraordinarily successful. By the age of thirty she had built a strong reputation on both sides of the Atlantic as a first-rate poet, the author of one very well-reviewed book of poems, *The Colossus*, and of many innovative and brilliant magazine-published poems. She had won so many awards, honors, and scholarships that it would take two pages to list them: poetry prizes in America and Britain, magazine prizes from *Mademoiselle* and *Seventeen*, a foundation grant, and a Fulbright. The BBC commissioned poetry readings and talks from her and produced her radio play *Three Women* in 1962. In 1963, the year of her death, her novel *The Bell Jar* was published in England. In what sense, then, can it be said that "her genius did not earn for her certain reprieves and comforts tendered the male artist"?

The obvious fact about Plath's literary career is that it provides no explanation for her suicide. It was a virtually uninterrupted string of successes from the time of her first published poem in 1950, "Bitter Strawberries," when she was seventeen, in the *Christian Science Monitor*. She was hardly out of high school when she won awards from *Mademoiselle* for her short stories. While she was at Smith College, her poetry was consistently recognized by the judges at poetry contests and by the editors of magazines. Her villanelles were accepted at *Harper's* while she was still in college; she won a poetry contest when she graduated; and she was published in a wide variety of magazines.

From 1955 to 1960, Plath continued to receive excellent responses to her work. Almost every poem that would eventually appear in *The Colossus* (1960) was first published in magazine form. Her years at Cambridge (1955–57) on a Fulbright and the two years in the United States (1957–59) prior to her permanent move to England were extremely productive. She wrote prose and poetry, including most of the poems now in *The Colossus* and *Lyonnesse*. She studied under Robert Lowell for a semester at Boston University and made significant changes in the style and material of her poems. It is true that she had trouble placing the manuscript of *The Colossus* with an American publishing house in 1958 and 1959, but she had a quick success with William Heinemann, Ltd., in April 1960.

Plath's years in England were difficult for her, but the problems cannot be attributed to persecution or neglect suffered at the hands of men. She found it difficult to produce more than a few poems a year, she said in 1961, although it should be remembered what personal events surrounded her creative work in England that year: a miscarriage; an appendectomy; a one-year-old child at home; and recurrent bouts of sinusitus. If she found her own literary success and achievements inadequate, then hers was a more severe judgment than anyone observing her career could have made. The only recognition that she lacked was internal; she could not believe that her success was both real and well-deserved.

It is simply inaccurate, then, to invoke the specter of a masculine "conspiracy" against Plath either during her life or after her death. She did not suffer from a critical or cultural neglect greater than that experienced by male poets in America. In fact, the similarity between Plath's fate and the self-destructive fate of such recent American male poets as Weldon Kees, John Berryman, Randall Jarrell, and Delmore Schwartz argues against the theory of her cultural victimization. The significant point about American poetry, which Chesler ignores, is not that women writers cannot gain equal acceptance with male writers, but that neither male nor female American poets gain much acceptance at all. The lack of public and material recognition does not explain the self-destructiveness of American poets, but it does suggest that both men and women poets are, with respect to the reception of their art, in much the same situation. It is absurd to claim that Plath would have been "saved" had she been a man, considering the fact that so many male poets have *not* been saved.

The argument that Plath possessed a feminist consciousness or adopted a political stance in regard to male-female relationships has only slightly more merit than the claim that she was victimized by men. Plath is not a feminist writer because she does not commit herself to ideological issues in her work. She does not express the notion that women are oppressed by men as a class nor does she suggest the need for action by women as a class against men. The rage expressed in the poems against men is directed, with certain exceptions, against specific individuals, her father and her husband or their symbolic representatives, not against men in general. The exceptions to this statement, found in "Lady Lazarus," "Purdah," "The Applicant," and several passages in *Three Women*, do not by themselves justify the idea that Plath had a feminist "politics." They indicate that in a few poems Plath generalized her rage against the fantasized image of her dead father and against her husband into an attack on marriage and men.

Yet in several poems, "Lesbos," "Medusa," and "The Other," Plath also directed her rage against women. Needless to say, she has not been labeled an antifeminist writer, even though these attacks upon women are only slightly less intense than her assault upon male figures in "Daddy" and "Lady Lazarus." When Plath quotes the words of her female friend in "Lesbos," she is mocking any bond that exists between one woman and another as a result of their common gender or shared oppression:

> Your voice my ear-ring,
> Flapping and sucking, blood-loving bat.
> That is that. That is that.
> You peer from the door,
> Sad hag. "Every woman's a whore.
> I can't communicate."
>
> [*A*, p. 32]

Significantly, one of Plath's recurrent images for women is the Medusa, the mythological creature who turns those who look at her into stone. In "Lesbos" and many of the other poems that speak of women, the negative presentations of women hardly support the view that Plath was even a proto-feminist writer.

The distinction between Plath's view of male-female relationships and a feminist view becomes clearer when she is compared with a writer like Virginia Woolf. Woolf's feminist position is stated in her prose works and expressed in her novels through the consistent attributions of certain opposed emotional qualities and attitudes to men and to women. Plath's attitude toward men and women is never stated in an ideological fashion in her prose; and the various contradictory perceptions of male and female situations in the poems suggest that she possessed no consistent viewpoint on this issue. Rather, she perceived both men and women at different moments as either supporting or harming the integrity of her self. The central issue in Plath's relation to others appears to have been the extent to which men or women embodied a threat to her existence. In certain poems, any other human being, independent of gender, seems to constitute a danger to the poet's life.

Plath did possess a consciousness of political issues, but the focus of her politics was neither women nor men's role in women's oppression. As she explained in a BBC interview, she was imaginatively involved in those historical-political events that were closest to the concerns voiced in her poems: Hiroshima and the A-bomb; Auschwitz and Nazism. In an article in the *London Magazine*, she refers to the danger inherent in the military-industrial complex, which had grown enormously in the late fifties, and in the development of nuclear armaments.[8] Since both the interview and the essay date from 1961–62, it is clear that Plath identified with political attitudes that were embodied in the peace movement of the early sixties. Again, nothing suggests that she had ideologized her own marital difficulties into a "case" against the masculine oppression of women.

Plath might, of course, have developed a feminist stance had she lived to see the development of the women's movement, but this is only hypothetical speculation. While she was alive, she clearly did not hold a feminist position, although her poems touch upon issues that would later become critical for feminist writers. For example, her strongest poems on the subject of marriage, "The Jailor," "Purdah," "Daddy," and

"The Applicant," speak of marriage as a form of imprisonment in which the woman either revolts against her entrapment by the man or suffers through it with a kind of ironic passivity. To read these poems as feminist tracts, however, is to supply an ideological structure for them that they do not possess. They dramatize personal struggles on the part of the various personae to free themselves of psychological dependency and self-hatred. They form part of Plath's drive toward self-transformation enacted by her poetry as a whole.

If we reject the simplistic notion of objective sexual oppression as the cause of Plath's suicide, we must also deny that her death resulted from heroic self-revelations of the poetry itself. This view has been most strongly argued by A. Alvarez in his study of suicide, *The Savage God*, although several other writers have adopted the same general position. Alvarez believes that the self-exposure and self-dramatization of *Ariel* and *Winter Trees* fatally exacerbated the psychological disturbances that eventually led to Plath's suicide. He presents a romantic view of a poet who heroically pursues the sources of her own inner torment, following Robert Lowell's lead in *Life Studies* (1959), until she is destroyed by her own quest for self-knowledge:

In the mass of brilliant poems which poured out in the last few months of her life she took Lowell's example to its logical conclusion, systematically exploring the nexus of anger, guilt, rejection, love and destructiveness, which made her finally take her own life. It is as though she had decided that for her poetry to be valid, it must tackle head-on nothing less serious than her own death, bringing to it a greater wealth of invention and sardonic energy than most poets manage in a lifetime of so-called affirmation.

If the road had seemed impassable, she proved that it wasn't. It was, however, one-way, and she went too far along it to be able, in the end, to turn back. Yet her actual suicide, like Lowell's breakdown or the private horrors of Berryman and Hughes, is incidental; it adds nothing to her work and proves nothing about it. *It was simply a risk that she took in handling such volatile material.*[9]

This conception of Plath's career is appealing until we examine it more deeply. Then Alvarez's view appears to be based on nothing more than a fervent desire to believe in art as a potentially self-destructive and, therefore, existential activity. Writing certainly involves commitments and risks that could be called "existential," but Plath's suicide was not the consequence of her commitment to "tackle head-on . . . her own death." Plath had been suicidal long before she dived into her unconscious through extremist poetry. In 1953 she attempted suicide in the basement of her mother's home in Wellesley, Massachusetts. Yet at that time she was composing poems that Alvarez has characterized as "formal" and "elegant," devoid of any commitment to personal risk. Alvarez suggests no link between the suicide attempt and these earlier poems because, obviously, there is none. Plath did not become suicidal because she wrote extremist verse in 1962–63. She had been obsessed with suicide from at least the period of her junior year at Smith in 1952–53; and the causes for her attraction to self-destruction undoubtedly go back to the shattered family situation of her childhood.

The similarities between Plath's suicide attempt in 1953 and her actual suicide in 1963 suggest, in fact, that her self-destruction was a response not to her literary activities but to a repetitive biographical situation. In the summer of 1953, Plath was faced with the prospect of separation from Smith the following year, with the loss of the security and approval that she had had at college, and with the end of her adolescence. Ten years later, she confronted a situation involving an even greater sense of loss and deprivation: she had lost her husband to another woman; she and her two children were living in a freezing, broken-down apartment in London; she had little sense of financial security; and her future was clouded by regrets over her broken marriage. While there are obvious differences in the two situations, the key link between them is Plath's despair over separation. In both cases she appears to have responded by turning to suicide as a complex solution to the overwhelming losses that were either about to occur or had already occurred.

Alvarez's linking of literature and suicide in Plath's case fails on obvious biographical grounds, but it is also inaccurate in terms of her relation to her own literary creativity. A reading of Plath's statements about poetry as well as of the poetry itself indicates that she saw literature as an essentially constructive activity. Alvarez talks about the "volatile material" that Plath could not handle safely, but Plath characterizes her poetry as a life-giving force that deals with the frightening realities of the modern world in terms of universal biological and creative processes. In her article in the *London Magazine* Plath wrote:

My poems do not turn out to be about Hiroshima, but about a child forming itself finger by finger in the dark. They are not about the terrors of mass extinction, but about the blackness of the moon over a yew tree in a neighbouring graveyard. . . . For me, the real issues of our time are the issues of every time—the hurt and wonder of loving; making in all its forms—children, loaves of bread, paintings, buildings; and the conservation of life of all people in all places.[10]

It is not accidental that Plath speaks here of her poetry in terms of children and childbirth. Throughout the last phase of her career she recurrently dramatized the process of birth and wrote numerous poems to her children. (She used birth as her central image of the life force in its struggle with death; and rebirth is the dominant personal objective of her later poems.) The specific dramatic movements of her work complete themselves in the violent assumption of a new shape or identity. When her poems seem inadequate to her, she speaks of them as stillborn children unable to enter life ("Stillborn"). Thus, although Alvarez's interpretation of the poetry suggests that the destructive and self-divisive aspects of art dominated Plath's imagination, actually the regenerative and integrative aspects appealed to Plath. Suicide is dramatized in the poems, yet it is the very opposite of the ultimate goal of rebirth that controls the development of image and idea in Plath's work.

Further, Plath clearly saw poetry as a necessary method of

controlling, rather than capitulating to, emotionally and psychologically disturbing material. In an interview for the BBC during the last year of her life, she claims that the artist's conscious manipulation of his own personal suffering is absolutely essential in good poetry:

I think my poems come immediately out of the sensuous and emotional experiences I have, but I must say I cannot sympathize with these cries from the heart that are informed by nothing except, you know, a needle or a knife, or whatever it is. I believe one should be able to control and manipulate experiences, even the most terrifying, like madness, like being tortured . . . and should be able to manipulate these experiences with an informed and intelligent mind.[11]

The "needle" or the "knife" were certainly present in Plath's imaginative experience, but Alvarez has precisely reversed the relation between that experience and her poetry. By controlling negative and terrifying experiences, Plath was able to order them in a psychically coherent and aesthetically satisfying form. The very effort to organize madness or terror provides the poet with a release from the inner pressures of self-destructive rage, guilt, or suffering. Control as well as psychic release are evident in the poems for which Plath is best known, "Daddy" and "Lady Lazarus." Although these poems have been criticized for their lack of control, they present a dramatic resolution to an explosive inner situation involving murderous and suicidal fantasies. Without such an ordering of these disturbing psychological situations, Plath might not have been able to adapt for as long as she did to the loneliness and despair of her last months alive.

To speak of Plath's poetry as the cause of her suicide, then, is to distort both the biographical and literary realities of her career in the service of a romantic legend. Several plausible explanations for Plath's suicide have been offered—as a revenge against her husband; as a means of reuniting in death with her father, who died when she was eight; and as a "cry for help."[12] But whatever the actual causes, her death took place in an atmosphere of misery and despair. It was not the victory of an artist who had followed her material wherever it would lead, even to her own destruction, but the defeat of a human being who found it impossible to suffer any longer the separation and isolation of her self. From Plath's childhood on, art had given her "a way of being happy," as she wrote in her childhood memoir "Ocean 1212-W." She was brought to suicide by pressures and forces that would ultimately be satisfied neither by art nor by any other human activity.

Plath's exploration of her personal world has led to a further misconception about her poetry that has dominated virtually every interpretation of her work. This view holds that her poems are examples of confessional verse and that they derive their form and structure from the private revelations made by the poet in her poems. The autobiographical daring of the late poems thus appears to many readers to constitute their essential novelty and importance. M. L. Rosenthal, who first applied the term *confession* to Robert Lowell's work, has argued that Plath followed Lowell's autobiographical method in *Life Studies*. Plath, he says, "chose, if that is the right word, the one alternative advance position to Lowell's along the dangerous confessional way, that of literally committing her own predicaments in the interests of her art until the one was so involved in the other that no return was possible." He goes on to claim that art and life are, in Plath's case, absolutely inseparable: "We shall never be able to sort out clearly the unresolved, unbearably exposed suggestibility and agitation of these poems from the purely aesthetic energy that shaped the best of them."[13] In *Sylvia Plath: Method and Madness*, Edward Butscher pursues this line of interpretation across the length of Plath's career. He attempts to show that Plath's confessionalism was the ultimate goal of her poetic career. The last poems, he says, express the "bitch goddess" within the poet and show her desire to "fuse biography in the late work with poetry to create an enduring legend."[14]

The confessional interpretation of Plath's work depends,

then, upon the notion that her art and life were so inseparably joined that one cannot talk about the poetry without discussing the biography. But this is untrue. The supposed inseparability of biography and poetry turns out to be nothing more than these critics' preference for biographical criticism. It is true that Plath's late poems derive almost entirely from the immediate experiences of her life: "Morning Song" and "Nick and the Candlestick" from incidents connected with her son; "Death & Co." from a visit in the hospital that she received from two acquaintances; "Cut" from a kitchen accident; "The Bee Meeting" from her beekeeping activities; "Tulips" from a convalescence after an operation; and "Ariel" from a horseback ride. But these works only begin with an autobiographical situation. As poems, they exist by themselves and can be read and understood in most cases without biographical information.

Furthermore, the label "confessional poetry" suggests that the poet has revealed his actual experience directly to his audience; Plath's literary strategy is quite different. She uses elements from her experience as the starting point for imagistic and thematic elaborations. The cries of her child, in "Morning Song," lead to a meditation on the essential separateness of the newborn from its parents; and the visit of friends in "Death & Co." allows her to objectify the contradictory faces of death. The poems offer revelations of fantasy, legend, and myth that support a body of related concerns. They do not terminate in the exposure of the poet's own psychological problems, but in the patterning of images around a few central themes.

Those who read Plath in confessional terms thus confuse the point of departure for the poems with their transformed and completed state. Plath's work, like that of many personal poets, is not merely autobiographical self-revelation, but reorders personal experience into patterns that obtain an objective character through repetition, allusion, and symbolic enactment. The personal elements in her work—the characters who are based upon her friends and relatives; the obsessive personal images of fear, love, and death; the autobiographical incidents

—serve the same function that the "impersonal" elements of history, politics, and myth do in other poetry. They provide an action and characters, define a setting, and generate a cluster of images and ideas. The action, characters, setting, and images then combine to form more than simply a portrait of the poet. Plath organizes them into a coherent dramatic plot.

The transformation of personal material through a dramatic setting gives Plath's work its significance. A body of poetry that simply exposes the poet's problems, daily interactions, and comments could be only a tedious form of narcissism. Plath's poetry suggests that the poet's experience is only the raw material with which he operates. A poem like "Ariel" possesses power and importance to the degree to which the horseback ride Plath once took becomes something more—a ride into the eye of the sun, a journey to death, a stripping of personality and selfhood. To treat "Ariel" as a confessional poem is to suggest that its actual importance lies in the horseride taken by its author, in the author's psychological problems, or in its position within the biographical development of the author. None of these issues is as significant as the imagistic and thematic developments rendered by the poem itself.

Even though many critics use the term *confessional* as a neutral label for a poetic movement, the word must indicate a narrowing of the range of literary possibility and achievement. Inevitably, confessionalism suggests that the writer has written so directly out of his personal experience and memory that he does not separate his autobiographical self from his projection in the poem. This sense of the term applies to many poets who rely on autobiography without any transforming or structuring principle in their poems. In much of Anne Sexton's poetry, for example, it is difficult to see how the impulse to self-revelation has been at all fashioned into a meaningful, self-sufficient aesthetic form. But this sort of confessionalism does not apply to Plath's work. Plath employs numerous personae; she establishes objective settings within which the speakers of her poems dramatize themselves; and she consistently employs imagery in a nonrealistic manner. Rather than using the personal image or autobiographical reference to reflect back upon herself, Plath uses personal allusions as the foundation for dramas of transformation and psychological process.

A final aspect of the general confessional interpretation of Plath should be mentioned. By linking her work to Robert Lowell's, critics have given the false impression that *Life Studies* and *Ariel* form part of the identical poetic movement and share a common aim. The truth is more complex. Lowell's *Life Studies* provided the initial impetus for Plath to project and rework her experiences of sickness and mental suffering. Lowell had dealt, in poems like "Waking in the Blue" and "Home after Three Months Away," with his life in and out of mental hospitals. His revelations of suffering and depression inevitably touched Plath closely: she had known him through his poetry course at Boston University, which she attended unofficially; she had spent time in the same mental hospital Lowell had; and she had already begun, following Roethke's example, to place greater emphasis in her poems upon personal material. Lowell spoke directly and realistically of father and mother, wife and friends. Plath wrote about Lowell's work: "I've been very excited by what I felt is the new breakthrough that came with Robert Lowell's *Life Studies*. This intense breakthrough into very serious, very personal emotional experience, which I feel has been partly taboo. Robert Lowell's poems about his experience in a mental hospital, for example, interest me very much."[15] In *Life Studies* she found a model of openness, both poetic and personal. Her experiences of mental derangement and dissociation could now be handled directly and personally. She could be "dauntless" and "reckless" in her admission of private material within the poems because Lowell had, in a sense, validated this approach to poetry.

Yet from the very beginning of Plath's transitional period (1960–61), her orientation was different from Lowell's. In *Crossing the Water* several of Plath's poems deal with hospital experiences, a subject Lowell had made famous; but they approach the subject on a different plane. In one of her more derivative poems, "Face Lift" (1961), Plath picks up the phrasing and tone of Lowell's "Waking in the Blue" ("Cock of the walk, / I strut in my turtle-necked French sailor's jersey"),[16] but she uses the hospital situation for different purposes:

Traveling

Nude as Cleopatra in my well-boiled hospital shift,
Fizzy with sedatives and unusually humorous,
I roll to an anteroom where a kind man
Fists my fingers for me. He makes me feel something precious
Is leaking from my finger-vents. At the count of two
Darkness wipes me out like chalk on a blackboard . . .
I don't know a thing.

[*CW*, p. 5; ellipsis points in text]

Lowell's poem focuses on the hospital attendant and on two mental patients, Stanley and "Bobbie," emphasizing the pathetic absurdity of the inmates ("I grin at Stanley, now sunk in his sixties, / once a Harvard all-American fullback") and the communal depression ("We are all old-timers, / each of us holds a locked razor"). Though Plath's poem is ostensibly about a woman having a face-lift, her images enter the inner world of the individual to a much greater depth than Lowell's. Lowell stays on the surface, observing, while Plath descends to the level at which identity forms and reforms itself. The speaker of "Face Lift" undergoes an inner change of identity: "For five days I lie in secret, / Tapped like a cask, the years draining into my pillow" (*CW*, p. 5). Having abandoned her old self in "some laboratory jar," she wakes "swaddled in gauze, / Pink and smooth as a baby" (*CW*, p. 6). The speaker's face-lift is actually a transformation of her personality. For Plath, a change in the speaker's inner world is, in effect, a change in reality; for Lowell the inner sphere of change is hardly touched in his consideration of reality.

When Plath attempts in *Crossing the Water* to imitate the

direct autobiographical style of *Life Studies*, the consequences
are unfortunate. In "The Babysitters" she uses a realistic Mas-
sachusetts background, like Lowell's in "Skunk Hour," and an
autobiographical situation:

> It is ten years, now, since we rowed to Children's Island.
> The sun flamed straight down that noon on the water off
>   Marblehead.
> That summer we wore black glasses to hide our eyes.
> We were always crying, in our spare rooms, little put-upon
>   sisters,
> In the two, huge, white, handsome houses in Swampscott.
> When the sweetheart from England appeared, with her cream
>   skin and Yardley cosmetics,
> I had to sleep in the same room with the baby on a too-short
>   cot,
> And the seven-year-old wouldn't go out unless his jersey
>   stripes
> Matched the stripes of his socks.
>
> [CW, p. 14]

"The Babysitters" is a dead end for Plath. Although the poetic
line has been opened up and the diction is now colloquial,
naming everyday objects (cosmetics, jersey stripes), the in-
tensity of the poem has been lost amid the external details.
What worked in "Skunk Hour" for Lowell fails utterly for
Plath in "The Babysitters."

The most fruitful line of her poetic development came not
from the autobiographical-realistic tendency in Lowell but
from the personal-imagistic focus of Plath's own mind. As
Marjorie Perloff has pointed out in her book on Lowell, *Life
Studies* uses a realistic technique to express Lowell's historical
concerns.[17] A specific memory of a family incident, of dead
family members, or of an important location gives the poems
in *Life Studies* their basic structure. Covering a period from the
1920s to the 1950s, *Life Studies* dramatizes Lowell's early rela-

tions to his father and mother, his jail experiences as a pacifist during World War II, events during his marriage, and his mental hospital visits. To accomplish this historical reconstruction, he must provide realistic information. From within the poems, we learn that he is the son of Commander Lowell, whose dates he gives us, whose occupation he analyzes, and whose life he dissects. Lowell is the boy who spent time with his Uncle Devereux Winslow in the summer of 1922. He is the man who was once, according to "Waking in the Blue," confined to McLean's Hospital. This kind of information does not appear in Plath's poetry. Lowell uses it because he is creating an art of historical portraiture in *Life Studies*, an art he develops even further in the four versions of *Notebook 1967–68* and in *The Dolphin*.

The disturbing personal feelings and thoughts in *Life Studies* appear, then, in an essentially historical and social context. The confessional material is almost always related to a memory of a previous moment in Lowell's life. We can see the movement from present to past, and from past to present, in "Grandparents":

> They're altogether otherworldly now,
> those adults champing for their ritual Friday spin
> to pharmacist and five-and-ten in Brockton.
> Back in my throw-away and shaggy span
> of adolescence, Grandpa still waves his stick
> like a policeman;
> Grandmother, like a Mohammedan, still wears her thick
> lavender mourning and touring veil;
> the Pierce Arrow clears its throat in a horse-stall.
> ·
> The farm's my own!
> Back there alone,
> I keep indoors, and spoil another season.
> I hear the rattley little country gramaphone
> racking its five foot horn:

"O Summer Time!"
Even at noon here the formidable
. *Ancien Régime* still keeps nature at a distance.[18]

Here is a poet living alternately in a rich historical past and a depressive present, relating his personal sense of the world through a juxtaposition of objective information: the five-and-ten store; Brockton, Massachusetts; the grandfather's cane; the touring veil; and the popular song. Lowell is a realist in *Life Studies*, a historically minded poet, who uses his own experience as a structuring device for his recollection of the past.

In contrast, Plath was strongly influenced by such poets as D. H. Lawrence, Dylan Thomas, and Theodore Roethke. Like those three, she was concerned with processes that go on underneath the surface of consciousness and yet affect the self in more intimate and powerful ways than do conscious processes. History, politics, and society appear in her work only tangentially. There is no sense, as there is in Lowell, of a historically situated personality "confessing" to a series of troubling, "real" experiences. Plath's poetry creates a space where the dramatic processes of self can be heard and seen without names, dates, and locations. As will be shown in Chapter 2, her mature poems consistently strive to reach the deep level where fundamental psychological change occurs. At this level in the psyche, every aspect of the body and mind is under the tremendous pressure of self-destructive and self-creative impulses.

The three states of Plath's career demonstrate her progress toward incorporating this life-and-death struggle within her own poetic forms. From 1950 through 1959 she spent much of her energy assimilating the language and forms of the Moderns, producing *The Colossus* by the end of this period. The following two years were transitional ones in which she moved hesitatingly toward more open forms and a new, personal language. The third and final stage encompassed the last year of her life, 1962–63, marked by the poems that now make up

Ariel, *Winter Trees*, and *Pursuit*. Throughout her career Plath demonstrated a striking ability to change styles and aesthetic attitudes with great rapidity. In fact, nothing better exemplifies the themes of transformation and inner change in her work than does her own remarkable transformation as a poet during her brief lifetime.

two

The Drama of Initiation

> *And she knew that her own private initiation*
> *had just begun.*[1]
>
> —"Initiation" (1953)

Sylvia Plath's importance in recent American poetry lies not in her exposure of autobiographical material, but in her dramatic approach to the representation of a threatened and violent self. Her mixed, violent world of nostalgia and hatred, of self-transformation and negation, would have little poetic force were it not for her conversion of ·fantasy and memory into dramatic expression and encounter. In the crucial year of change in her career, 1959, Plath came to realize that purely lyric methods could not adequately represent her sense of the antagonism between herself and others and that this antagonistic relationship must be rendered through a dramatic heightening of her own speaking voice. This recognition eventually led to the poems that have been responsible for Plath's posthumous reputation and for her large influence upon contemporary poetry. Collected mainly in *Ariel* and *Winter Trees*, these works testify to Plath's ability to capture the self in a series of extraordinary poses: in relation to its own birth and death, to physical mutilation, to children, and to the family. The very limitation of thematic concern in Plath's work helps to concentrate and to intensify the dramatic conflict with others. As she worked out the implications of using dramatic methods in lyric poetry, she deepened her approach to the themes of initiation.

To speak of Plath's work in terms of a dramatic principle is to encompass those methods in her late work that bring the speaker into contact with the Other. The personae in her poems speak to a wide variety of listeners, thus dramatizing a struggle with both human and natural forces. They speak to other people, often a child or family member; to quasi-mythological figures, often invented by the poet: the Rival, the Other, Medusa; to nonhuman objects: bees or a tree; or even to a split-off part of the poet's body or self. Plath may use direct address, as in her dramatic monologues, or invocation; or she may split the narrator's personality into different parts, simulating an interior dialogue. Whatever the poetic form, her intention is clearly to find a voice and a situation that will externalize the internal, conflicting agencies of her personality.

Using methods that are midway between lyric and drama, Plath dramatizes a ritual confrontation with a powerful enemy force: either death and its symbolic agents or life and its harsh demands for self-negation and painful individuation. This meeting between self and destructive other occurs frequently in a symbolic space that is often reached through a journey or voyage. In this central place those aspects of existence that consciousness normally separates and opposes come together as one. Death and birth, self and other, good and evil, merge in a kind of darkness. Frequently, Plath compares this darkness to that of the womb, suggesting that she wishes to imitate the condition of unity that existed before the differentiation of consciousness took place in childhood. She gives a good account of this regressive tendency in her childhood memoir, "Ocean 1212-W," in which the sea is said to have been both a nurturing and a terrifying "mother" for her:

Breath, that is the first thing. Something is breathing. My own breath? The breath of my mother? No, something else, something larger, farther, more serious, more weary. So behind shut lids I float awhile;—I'm a small sea captain, tasting the day's weather—battering rams at the seawall, a spray of grapeshot on my mother's brave geraniums, or the lulling shoosh-shoosh of a full mirrory pool; the pool turns the quartz grits at its rim idly and kindly, a lady brooding at jewellery. There might be a hiss of rain on the pane, there might be wind sighing and trying the creaks of the house like keys. I was not deceived by these. The motherly pulse of the sea made a mock of such counterfeits. Like a deep woman, it hid a good deal; it had many faces, many delicate, terrible veils. It spoke of miracles and distances; if it could court, it could also kill.[2]

In its juxtaposition of the opposed qualities of the sea, this passage mirrors the violently contrasting attitudes that the poems take toward a series of crucial, related terms: the sea, mother, nature, and, ultimately, life. Plath consistently finds in her adult relation to the external world the same opposition she had discovered as a child in her "filial" relation to the sea. The world, like the sea, has "delicate" veils that are simultaneously "terrible" veils, as she showed in a late poem, "A Birthday Present." Like the sea, the world both "courts," suggesting the seductions of a sexual encounter, and "kills," indicating a fatal mixture of death and sexuality, as Plath would later demonstrate in the double-faced vision of death in "Death & Co." The journey to the center of life is, in Plath's work, the same as the journey to death; both return her to the sea, to her mother, and therefore to the earliest stages of her life, when the boundaries between being and nonbeing hardly existed.

Two alternatives emerge as a result of Plath's attraction to her origins and her frequent symbolic journeys backward and inward to the beginning of life. The darkness into which the poet or persona enters may be the prelude to death or it may provide the means to gain a more vivid and compelling life. These two opposed consequences of abandoning the intellectual and physical status of adulthood provide the dynamic basis for Plath's poetry. She often takes the reader into a vortex of energies that produces either survival and new life or destruction and death, depending upon the forces that gain control of consciousness. Her poems dramatize a personality's struggle for continuing existence as it survives repeated encounters with death.

Plath's poetry can thus be seen as a ritual action that defines the roles the poet and her personae may play. The aspects of the poetry that best define its ritual character are the sequence of stages or steps Plath pursues on the way to a psychological or physical self-transformation; the interpenetration of death and birth in the thematic structure; the repetition of a particular kind of symbolic setting, as in the preestablished scenes of a rite; the recurrence of the same symbolically charged image sequences; and the belief in demonic and spirit forms. Taken together, these elements compose a poetry of initiation in which the self and the body are transformed through a succession of profound changes. The initiatory character of the work emerges most clearly when we realize how closely Plath follows the structural pattern and imagery of initiatory practices in archaic societies.

The historian of religions, Mircea Eliade, who is the best guide to the structure of initiatory myth and ritual, offers a persuasive interpretation of what he calls the "scenario of initiation."[3] According to Eliade, archaic man places a positive value on death through the initiation rite, during which he simulates his own dying. By willingly undergoing physical mutilation (as in circumcision and subincision rites), symbolic dismemberment, and symbolic death, the initiate passes through death on the way to rebirth and a new life. The pattern of death and rebirth is so common in the ritual practices and the literature of all cultures, including modern ones, that Eliade feels free to call initiation the fundamental method that men have developed in order to deal with dying. Men solicit and engage death so as to overcome it. Initiatory death, in Eliade's view, is

indispensable for the beginning of spiritual life. Its function must be understood in relation to what it prepares: birth to a higher mode of being. . . . Initiatory death is often symbolized, for example, by darkness, by cosmic night, by the telluric womb, the hut, the belly of a monster. All these images express regression to a preformal state, to a latent mode of being . . . rather than total annihilation. . . . These images and symbols of ritual death are inextricably connected with germination, with embryology; they already indicate a new life in preparation.[4]

If Eliade's perceptions about initiation are adapted to Plath's work, it becomes clear that her poems frequently perceive of death not as a suicidal ending but as the path to a transformed identity. This point is of particular importance because the common critical tendency is to view Plath solely as a poet of suicide.[5] Actually, her imagery and the characteristic movement of her poems dramatize a death-and-rebirth pattern in much the same way that her novel, *The Bell Jar*, embodies a psychic death and regeneration. In a central group of poems, including "The Stones, "Lady Lazarus," "Ariel," and "Fever 103°," the transformation of death into life follows the three-part structure that most students of myth see as basic to initiation: entry into darkness, ritual death, and rebirth.[6] Most of Plath's late poems dramatize only one or two of these aspects of initiatory structure, but almost all of them use the setting and imagery of ritual action. The dominant pattern of Plath's work—the journey to a black space, where all opposites become one—merges at key moments into the larger action of initiation. Plath never attained a secure identity through the imitation of initiation, but her poetry reaches out toward the fulfillment promised by ritual.

The three-part initiatory scenario in Plath's poetry can perhaps be best demonstrated by showing the imagistic and thematic elements that pertain to each stage in a number of poems. The first stage in the initiatory process involves the transformation of the external setting of the poem—landscape, seascape, domestic or hospital scene—into a symbolic world of death. In "Tulips" (1961), for example, the monologue is spoken by a woman in a hospital bed. Recovering from surgery, she thinks of her hospital room as a white sea of death in which her body is a pebble. The monologue substitutes the metaphoric reality of water, pebbles, and cargo boats for the actuality of the hospital. The initial stage of change in "Tulips," then, places the self in a watery space where she can die.

Similarly, in "The Jailor," the external scene is immediately transformed into a symbolic map of death. The kitchen setting becomes a stage for torture as the Jailor wheels in "properties" representing death: "The same placard of blue fog is wheeled into position / With the same tree and headstones."[7] "The Moon and the Yew Tree" begins by redefining the landscape in terms of deathly coldness and alienation. The moon's light becomes "the light of the mind, cold and planetary" (*A*, p. 41). The speaker in "The Arrival of the Bee Box" changes the box immediately into an emblem of death: "I would say it was the coffin of a midget / Or a square baby" (*A*, p. 59). Almost all of Plath's poems demonstrate the initial metaphorical transformation of the environment into the world of death.

Parallel symbolic settings are therefore a constant element in the process enacted by the poetry. Whether the poems take place inside a house or in the countryside, the identical metaphorical relationships are established between a vulnerable speaker and a destructive environment. In "A Birthday Present," the setting for the encounter with death is a kitchen; in "The Rabbit Catcher," it is a country path near the sea. Yet the objects upon which Plath focuses embody the same death force. In one case, the birthday present itself introduces the chilling, suffocating power of mortality; in the other, it is the sea and the wind. "The Rabbit Catcher" shows the wind "gagging" the speaker's mouth and "tearing off" her voice, the sea "blinding" her as she sees the "lives of the dead" unreeling in the water. "A Birthday Present" symbolizes death through an image of veils:

Now there are these veils, shimmering like curtains,

The diaphanous satins of a January window
White as babies' bedding and glittering with dead breath. O
    ivory!

[A, p. 42]

Whiteness, as in "Tulips," symbolizes the dead world, blocking our awareness of life. Death has thus embedded itself both in the sea and in the veiled birthday gift, completing the initial movement toward the darkness.

In the second stage, the individual undergoes drastic self-transformation in order to escape from the violence of the death world. Paradoxically, this escape takes the form of physical destruction, including self-mutilation, dismemberment, or symbolic annihilation. The adult body comes apart and loses its physical integrity under the pressure of violence that may be directed by others against the self or by the self against its own body. This process may be experienced as either pleasurable or painful, depending upon the psychic motive that accompanies the particular image or action. Plath often switches from a horrified awareness of disintegration to an intense longing for it. In "The Bee-Meeting," for instance, the symbolic embodiment of the speaker's own death in a bee-box terrifies her: "Whose is that long white box in the grove, what have they accomplished, why am I cold?" (*A*, p. 58). Contrastingly, in "Tulips," the self wishes to throw off her life, with its attachments to others and the weight of its sorrow and guilt. Her death is now imagined as a return to the womb, as she sees herself blissfully undergoing the last rites and sinking into water.

These opposed reactions to death are actually aspects of the same ritual descent into darkness. In poems like "Lady Lazarus" and "Fever 103°," which dramatize the complete destruction of personality and body, Plath expresses both attitudes. The speakers are simultaneously terrified by their annihilation and exalted by it. By bringing death and birth into the closest proximity, the process of initiation releases profoundly contradictory feelings toward existence. On the one hand, Plath seeks her own death because life appears unbearable, guilt-ridden, and worthless; on the other hand, she seeks death because it can give her new life by releasing the reservoir of love that will refresh the self. In the initiatory imagination, the self must be violently purged, usually through the assumption of a fetal or infantile condition, before it can take on a new identity. Evidently, the strategy of ritual is to use the death impulses to generate a renewed desire to live.

The characteristic imagery of this second stage in Plath's poems centers on physical dissolution and dismemberment. Her poems frequently employ images of knives, operations, amputations, blood, lost limbs, and cutting. Often she imagines herself being absorbed or "eaten" by some powerful force external to her, usually the darkness of the sky or water or of God. These images and processes point, of course, to the characteristic elements of initiations, with their bloodletting, incisions, and symbolic deaths. The poems appear to enact the various forms of mutilation and death, as in "Cut," "Death & Co.," and "The Detective," to control these feared eventualities. However, Plath never offers us an image that has only a single emotional charge or value. The imagery of disintegration is both fascinating and horrifying. In "Totem," the universe appears as a voracious mouth that consumes its own body: the railroad track "eaten" by the engine; the pigs and hares eaten by the farmers; men roped in and eaten by the spider Death. Absorption is a frightening prospect in "Totem." But in "Poppies in July," images of the mouth and of eating indicate a desirable state of being. Plath embraces the bloody mouth of the red poppies and wishes to become like them: "If I could bleed, or sleep!— / If my mouth could marry a hurt like that!" (*A*, p. 81). Death can be either self-laceration or salvation, agony or peacefulness.

The final stage of Plath's initiatory scenario occurs only when the body has been purged through its own annihilation or effacement. In "Face Lift," the operation on the persona culminates in the replacement of her old, hated face with a new one. Symbolically, the speaker gains a new self; she thus can triumphantly conclude: "Mother to myself, I wake swaddled in gauze, / Pink and smooth as a baby" (*WT*, p. 6). She has been able to perform the magical act of self-generation, which is the true goal of Plath's scenarios. After the ritual ordeal of dismemberment and dissolution, the self emerges as if reborn into a new world. Death is converted into new birth through an imitation of gestation and delivery: the reborn individual now possesses the innocence and freshness characteristic of an infant.

Imagery associated with this stage naturally revolves around birth and children. Embryological and obstetric metaphors predominate in poems that dramatize the rebirth of the self. In "Getting There," the speaker travels on a train across a landscape filled with the war-wounded, amputees, and the corpses of men and women. The world of the poem is a biological holocaust and appears to offer only one escape: the "bloodspot" at the end of the journey, where death and life converge. In this ritual space, the speaker hopes that the dead will be forgotten. Terrified of her situation, she determines on a ritual method of "getting there": "I shall bury the wounded like pupas, / I shall count and bury the dead." Since the pupa is the quiescent stage in an insect's life cycle, the reference suggests the possibility of renewed life, and it is this renewal that the speaker finally achieves for herself. She throws off her "old faces," as the speaker in "Face Lift" rejects her unwanted face and as the insect sheds its prior form, and she assumes a new body. The train of death turns magically into a carriage; the speaker steps "from the black car of Lethe, / Pure as a baby." The descent into hell, with its dismembered bodies and bloody battles, ends in innocence.

We can hardly read "Getting There," or any of the other late poems about birth and death, without feeling Plath's immense terror at biological reality. "Getting There" makes reference to the Krupp armament makers, to "some war or other," but its essential imagistic components are the dismemberment and destruction of the body, followed by its renewal. The intensity of Plath's drive toward self-transformation thus reflects her sense of entrapment in a body that, at any moment, might be hurt or damaged. From a clinical point of view, this obsession can be viewed as purely pathological; but the movement toward physical death is simultaneously a negation and an affirmation of self in Plath's poetry. In the full-scale dramas of initiation, Plath links death and birth so closely that they are virtually indistinguishable. The final image of "A Birthday Present" combines references to cutting and to birth. The speaker has been asking for an appropriate "birthday" gift— her death: "And the knife not carve, but enter / Pure and clean as the cry of a baby" (*A*, p. 44). The deadly irony of the punning title suggests that only death could satisfy the speaker, but the final image gives another dimension to the death-wish: Plath wants to go back to the purity of infancy as an alternative to the agonizing present. The return to childhood is a cleansing, or purging, experience, just as death in "Getting There" prepares the speaker for a return to life.

"Ariel" also employs the image of the crying child to indicate the reduction of self to its original, preadult state: "The child's cry / Melts in the wall" (*A*, p. 27). However, "Ariel" goes even further than "Getting There" in imagining a radical change in physical shape for the speaker. Having thrown off her body and dissolved the self according to the characteristic stages of the ritual journey, the speaker is resurrected as a nonhuman energy traveling across space:

> And I
> Am the arrow,
>
> The dew that flies
> Suicidal, at one with the drive
> Into the red
>
> Eye, the cauldron of morning.

The transformation of the self into water (dew) that will eventually be burned up in the solar furnace identifies the poet with the basic creative and destructive elements of the universe, water and fire. The ritual change thus becomes a cosmic journey to the source of life energy on the earth. By allowing the speaker to abandon her unwanted body, the uncontrolled horseride gives her the power of an arrow shot toward the sun.

The initiatory drama received its first extended treatment in "The Stones," which provides a good example of Plath's handling of the images and stages that would later be developed in *Ariel* and *Winter Trees*. It also suggests very strongly that Plath consciously chose to develop the themes of initiation and transformation at this crucial point in her career. Written in the fall of 1959 as the final poem of a seven-part sequence, "Poem for a Birthday," "The Stones" owes its origin to two sources: Theodore Roethke's poetry and Paul Radin's collection of African folktales.

Plath had been reading Roethke's poetry intensively in 1959.[8] She had imitated his manner of representing animal and vegetative existence in the earlier poems of the seven-part sequence. "Poem for a Birthday" imagines many bizarre transformations of personality. The speaker in "Maenad" becomes an unspecified creature: a "Dog-head, devourer" (*CW*, p. 51). In "Dark House" the indeterminate "I" makes a journey underground, like a mole, and discovers his "cuddly mother" inside the tunnels of the earth. These fantastic personae, like Roethke's narrators, become someone or something else: "I am becoming another," says the Maenad. The witch in "Witch Burning" loses her "shape" and goes up in flames. Plath's obsession in these works with animals, eating, mothers, and transformation derives directly from such Roethke poems as "Unfold! Unfold!" and "Praise to the End!" The associations of Roethke's "I Need, I Need" appear to have influenced her:

> A deep dish. Lumps in it.
> I can't taste my mother.
> Hoo. I know the spoon.
> Sit in my mouth.[9]

The first six poems of Plath's sequence are written in this obscure Roethkian idiom; "The Stones" is rooted in a more recognizable and realistic action. It brings Roethke's concern with transformation and the interior life onto the level of a discernible, though metaphorically altered, human situation.

The central reason for this change is the influence on "The Stones" of Paul Radin's *African Folktales and African Sculpture*.[10] An anthropologist, Radin brought together a number of African myths and tales under such categories as "The Universe and Its Beginnings," "The Animal and His World," and "Man and His Fate." Prominent in the collection are tales about caterpillars, elephants, and spiders who embody certain archetypal themes: the discovery of evil; the dangers of jealousy; the struggle between good and evil. These tales, involving magical powers and sudden transformations, must have appealed to a writer who had herself extensively used animals and animal fables in the poems that would eventually make up *The Colossus* ("The Bull of Bendylaw," "Metamorphosis," "Blue Moles," "Sow," "Frog Autumn," "Flute Notes from a Reedy Pond," "Snakecharmer"). Radin's stories seemed ready-made for Plath's use.

One of Radin's tales directly influenced the structure of "The Stones." "The City Where Men Are Mended" provided the basic idea for the poem as well as a key phrase.[11] The story deals with an evil wife's attempt to outdo a rival wife, who had a beautiful daughter. When the good wife's daughter is killed by a hyena, nothing remains but the girl's bones. The mother is told, however, that if she brings these bones to the "city where men are mended," the girl will be returned to life. Because the woman is good, the prophecy comes true; her beautiful daughter is revived and reconstructed. Learning of this wondrous event, the evil wife imagines that she, too, can benefit from the "city where men are mended." The bad mother determines to kill her own ugly daughter and take the girl's bones to the city, hoping for a cosmetic improvement. She puts her daughter in a mortar, pounds her up, and then carries the bones to the city. Of course, the evil mother does not get her wish: her daughter returns from the city even more hideous than she had been prior to her death, reconstructed with only one leg, one buttock, one hand, and one side to her body.

This archaic tale of mothers and daughters, death and re-birth, must have struck Plath for its simple statement of the relationship between her central obsessive concern: the terror of physical mutilation and the possibility of self-renewal. Plath begins "The Stones" when the speaker is already within the walls of the magical city:

> This is the city where men are mended.
> I lie on a great anvil.
> The flat blue sky-circle
>
> Flew off like the hat of a doll
> When I flew out of the light. I entered
> The stomach of indifference, the wordless cupboard.
>
> The mother of pestles diminished me.
> I became a still pebble.
> The stones of the belly were peaceable,
>
> The head-stone quiet, jostled by nothing.
> Only the mouth-hole piped out,
> Importunate cricket.
>
> [C, p. 82]

The opening line identifies the location of the poem, the African city of transformation; but not until the third stanza do we learn the identity of the speaker. She is not, as might be expected, the good mother's beautiful daughter; she is the ugly daughter of the evil mother, "The mother of pestles," who has ground the daughter down to bone. Plath has taken certain liberties with the original tale: the daughter's crushed bones have become stone; the girl has come to the "city" for the conversion of stone into flesh rather than the reconstruction of shattered bones. But the transformative goal of the poem and the folktale are identical. Both imagine a magical altera-tion in the constitution of a woman's body. Both dramatize a daughter's salvation from a world of hardness and death.

"The Stones" goes on, though, to work out a full-scale

initiatory pattern for the speaker. The images in the first few stanzas recall the perceptions of a child: the sky is like "the hat of a doll"; the "wordless cupboard" suggests a nursery-rhyme image. The self returns to a world of childhood in which metaphors exclusively determine reality. The body petrifies into stone, and familiar objects are transformed. A table, for instance, becomes a "great anvil." The setting of the poem prepares for the initiatory ordeal by transforming the objects around the self—the sky, the city, the body, the stomach—into symbolic agents of death. Every element in the poem forms part of the mythic setting that allows transformation to occur.

The second movement of the poem goes back past childhood to the condition of the fetus in the womb. The hardness and separateness of the stone body, with its stone eyes, stone mouth, and stone organs, resembles the protective body of the mother carrying the child. Inside the womb, the speaker is as isolated and happy as a fetus: "Drunk as a fetus," she says, "I suck at the paps of darkness." Combining the condition of the fetus in the womb with that of the infant at the mother's breasts, the speaker has given up her adulthood entirely. Eliade speaks of reembryonization as a universal aspect of initiation.[12] Certainly Plath provides numerous indications in this and other poems that she deliberately imagines such returns to the womb as steps toward a more comprehensive self-transformation. Petrification of the body precedes the emergence of new life.

Finally, the poem brings the speaker back from the womb-like state. The initiate is pulled out of her stony womb by the "jewelmasters," who chip at her hard body. Like doctors pulling the newborn from the mother's body, the jewelmasters preside over the birth of the new self. The embryological metaphor, which is central to initiatory practice, is fully dramatized: "This is the city of spare parts. / My swaddled legs and arms smell sweet as rubber." After the petrified body has been thrown off, the speaker can assume a new one, "swaddled" like a newborn. Like the daughter of the good wife in "The City Where Men are Mended," the speaker has been magically returned to life with a new and beautiful body. The poem begins by identifying the speaker with the deformed daughter of the evil mother and concludes with the characteristic "happy ending" of the initiatory scenario.

There is an obvious parallel between the experience recounted in "The Stones" and Plath's experience with electroshock therapy after her suicide attempt in 1953. The "City Where Men are Mended" is not only the mythical city of transformation but also the hospital in which she was treated for depression. The "current" that "agitates the wires / Volt upon volt" when the new body is grafted onto the old suggests the equipment of shock therapy; the jewelmasters appear to be psychiatrists. Yet the autobiographical background has no real presence in the poem. What matter are the dramatic alterations that occur as the speaker progressively describes her "operation" and the shifting images that flow through her consciousness. The imagery of "The Stones" is typical of Plath's poetry in its use of stone and pebbles to indicate the world of death and of babies and childbirth to signal the presence of life. Through these sequences of images Plath dramatizes the metaphoric conversion that lies at the basis of initiation: the generation of life from death.

"The Stones" is not, however, one of Plath's very best poems. Its metaphoric structure is developed in a linear, predictable manner; and the phrasing often degenerates into doggerel, as in the last lines: "My mendings itch. There is nothing to do. / I shall be good as new." In *Ariel* and *Winter Trees*, Plath escaped from both these evils: the overexplicit statement of metaphorical relationship and the awkward handling of colloquial phrases. In "Lady Lazarus" (October 1962), her handling of language and metaphor is much more versatile. The poem reflects Plath's recognition at the end of her life that the struggle between self and others and between death and birth must govern every aspect of the poetic structure. The magical and demonic aspects of the world appear in "Lady Lazarus" with an intensity that is absent from "The Stones."

The Lady of the poem is a quasi-mythological figure, a parodic version of the biblical Lazarus whom Christ raised from the dead. As in "The Stones," the speaker undergoes a series of transformations that are registered through image sequences. The result is the total alteration of the physical body. In "Lady Lazarus," however, the transformations are more violent and more various than in "The Stones," and the degree of self-dramatization on the part of the speaker is much greater. Four basic sequences of images define the Lady's identity. At the beginning of the poem, she is cloth or material: lampshade, linen, napkin; in the middle, she is only body: knees, skin and bone, hair; toward the end, she becomes a physical object: gold, ash, a cake of soap; finally, she is resurrected as a red-haired demon. Each of these states is dramatically connected to an observer or observers through direct address: first, to her unnamed "enemy"; then, to the "gentlemen and ladies"; next, to the Herr Doktor; and, finally, to Herr God and Herr Lucifer. The address to these "audiences" allows Plath to characterize Lady Lazarus's fragmented identities with great precision. For example, a passage toward the end of the poem incorporates the transition from a sequence of body images (scars-heart-hair) to a series of physical images (opus-valuable-gold baby) as it shifts its address from the voyeuristic crowd to the Nazi Doktor:

> And there is a charge, a very large charge,
> For a word or a touch
> Or a bit of blood
>
> Or a piece of my hair or my clothes.
> So, so, Herr Doktor.
> So, Herr Enemy.

I am your opus,
I am your valuable,
The pure gold baby

That melts to shriek.

[A, p. 8]

The inventiveness of the language demonstrates Plath's ability to create, as she could not in "The Stones," an appropriate oral medium for the distorted mental states of the speaker. The sexual pun on "charge" in the first line above; the bastardization of German ("Herr Enemy"); the combination of Latinate diction ("opus," "valuable") and colloquial phrasing ("charge," "So, so . . .")—all these linguistic elements reveal a character who has been grotesquely split into warring selves. Lady Lazarus is a different person for each of her audiences, and yet none of her identities is bearable for her. For the Nazi Doktor, she is a Jew, whose body must be burned; for the "peanut-crunching crowd," she is a stripteaser; for the medical audience, she is a wonder, whose scars and heartbeat are astonishing; for the religious audience, she is a miraculous figure, whose hair and clothes are as valuable as saints' relics. And when she turns to her audience in the middle of the poem to describe her career in suicide, she becomes a self-conscious performer. Each of her deaths, she says, is done "exceptionally well. / I do it so it feels like hell."

The entire symbolic procedure of death and rebirth in "Lady Lazarus" has been deliberately chosen by the speaker. She enacts her death repeatedly in order to cleanse herself of the "million filaments" of guilt and anguish that torment her. After she has returned to the womblike state of being trapped in her cave, like the biblical Lazarus, or of being rocked "shut as a seashell," she expects to emerge reborn in a new form. These attempts at rebirth are unsuccessful until the end of the poem. Only when the Lady undergoes total immolation of self and body does she truly emerge in a demonic form. The doctor burns her down to ash, and then she achieves her rebirth:

> Out of the ash
> I rise with my red hair
> And I eat men like air.

Using the phoenix myth of resurrection as a basis, Plath imagines a woman who has become pure spirit rising against the imprisoning others around her: gods, doctor, men, and Nazis. This translation of the self into spirit, after an ordeal of mutilation, torture, and immolation, stamps the poem as the dramatization of the basic initiatory process.

"Lady Lazarus" defines the central aesthetic principles of Plath's late poetry. First, the poem derives its dominant effects from the colloquial language. From the conversational opening ("I have done it again") to the clipped warnings of the ending ("Beware / Beware"), "Lady Lazarus" appears as the monologue of a woman speaking spontaneously out of her pain and psychic disintegration. The Latinate terms ("annihilate," "filaments," "opus," "valuable") are introduced as sudden contrasts to the essentially simple language of the speaker. The obsessive repetition of key words and phrases gives enormous power to the plain style used throughout. As she speaks, Lady Lazarus seems to gather up her energies for an assault on her enemies, and the staccato repetitions of phrases build up the intensity of feelings:

> I do it so it feels like hell.
> I do it so it feels real.
> I guess you could say I've a call.
>
> It's easy enough to do it in a cell.
> It's easy enough to do it and stay put.

This is language poured out of some burning inner fire, though it retains the rhythmical precision that we expect from a much less intensely felt expression. It is also a language made up almost entirely of monosyllables. Plath has managed to adapt a heightened conversational stance and a colloquial idiom to the dramatic monologue form.

The colloquial language of the poem relates to its second major aspect: its aural quality. "Lady Lazarus" is meant to be read aloud. To heighten the aural effect, the speaker's voice modulates across varying levels of rhetorical intensity. At one moment she reports on her suicide attempt with no observable emotion:

> I am only thirty.
> And like the cat I have nine times to die.
> This is Number Three.

The next moment she becomes a barker at a striptease show:

> Gentlemen, ladies,
> These are my hands.

Then she may break into a kind of incantatory chant that sweeps reality in front of it, as at the very end of the poem. The deliberate rhetoric of the poem marks it as a set-piece, a dramatic tour de force, that must be heard to be truly appreciated. Certainly it answers Plath's desire to create an aural medium for her poetry.

Third, "Lady Lazarus" transforms a traditional stanzaic pattern to obtain its rhetorical and aural effects. One of the striking aspects of Plath's late poetry is its simultaneous dependence on and abandonment of traditional forms. The three-line stanza of "Lady Lazarus" and such poems as "Ariel," "Fever 103°," "Mary's Song," and "Nick and the Candlestick" refer us inevitably to the terza rima of the Italian tradition and to the terza rima experiments of Plath's earlier work. But the poems employ this stanza only as a general framework for a variable-beat line and variable rhyming patterns. The first stanza of the poem has two beats in its first line, three in its second, and two in its third; but the second has a five-three-two pattern. The iambic measure is dominant throughout, though Plath often overloads a line with stressed syllables or reduces a line to a single stress. The rhymes are mainly off-rhymes ("again," "ten"; "fine," "linen"; "stir," "there"). Many of the pure rhymes are used to accentuate a bizarre conjunction of meaning, as in the lines addressed to the doctor: "I turn and burn. / Do not think I underestimate your great concern."

Finally, "Lady Lazarus," like "Daddy" and "Fever 103°," incorporates historical material into the initiatory and imagistic patterns. This element of Plath's method has generated much misunderstanding, including the charge that her use of references to Nazism and to Jewishness is inauthentic.[13] Yet these allusions to historical events form part of the speaker's fragmented identity and allow Plath to portray a kind of eternal victim. The very title of the poem lays the groundwork for a semicomic historical and cultural allusiveness. The Lady is a legendary figure, a sufferer, who has endured almost every variety of torture. Plath can thus include among Lady Lazarus's characteristics the greatest contemporary examples of brutality and persecution: the sadistic medical experiments on the Jews by Nazi doctors and the Nazis' use of their victims' bodies in the production of lampshades and other objects. These allusions, however, are no more meant to establish a realistic historic norm in the poem than the allusions to the striptease are intended to establish a realistic social context. The references in the poem—biblical, historical, political, personal—draw the reader into the center of a personality and its characteristic mental processes. The reality of the poem lies in the convulsions of the narrating consciousness. The drama of external persecution, self-destructiveness, and renewal, with both its horror and its grotesque comedy, is played out through social and historical contexts that symbolize the inner struggle of Lady Lazarus.

The claim that Plath misuses a particular historical experience is thus incorrect. She shows how a contemporary consciousness is obsessed with historical and personal demons and how that consciousness deals with these figures. The demonic characters of the Nazi Doktor and of the risen Lady Lazarus are surely more central to the poem's tone and intent than is the historicity of these figures. By imagining the initiatory drama against the backdrop of Nazism, Plath is universalizing a personal conflict that is treated more narrowly in such poems as "The Bee-Meeting" and "Berck-Plage." The fact that Plath herself was not Jewish has no bearing on the legitimacy of her employment of the Jewish persona: the holocaust serves her as a metaphor for the death-and-life battle between the self and a deadly enemy. Whether Plath embodies the enemy as a personal friend, a demonic entity, a historical figure, or a cosmic force, she consistently sees warfare in the structural terms of the initiatory scenario. "Lady Lazarus" is simply the most powerful and successful of the dramas in which that enemy appears as the sadistic masculine force of Nazism.

The persistence and depth of the initiatory images and structures in Plath's works point to the archaic nature of her beliefs, particularly her faith in spirit life and animism. Plath conceived of all life as endowed with consciousness or spirit. Animals, insects, and vegetation in her poetry are aware of their roles and take on characteristics that are normally reserved for human beings: a bull rises up against a kingdom ("The Bull of Bendylaw"); bees take revenge against their keepers ("Stings"); flowers suffer or feel pleasure ("Poppies in July"). "The world is blood-hot and personal" (*A*, p. 75), she says in one of her very last poems, in a phrase that could stand as the motto for all of her poetry. All organic life appears to Plath to live and die aware of its suffering and conscious of the violence or victimization that is part of nature.

The "personal" nature of the world thus imposes on all sentient beings the constant burden of suffering and death. Each encounter between beings and the world is a ritual confrontation with death that is repeated on all levels of existence and in all activities. For Plath death is a kind of spirit or god who incarnates himself in the objects and forms of the world: a man visiting her in the hospital, with lidded eyes, a "scald scar of water," and voracious desires; a father who bites his daughter's heart in two; a priest in his cassock and black shoes; manne-

quins in the shop windows of a dark Munich street; a black
yew tree moving in the wind, recalling the dead father; God,
inert and terrifying in his black heaven. At every turn death
appears to frighten and to seduce animal and man.

It is not surprising, then, that blood becomes Plath's symbol
both for animate beings and for a poetry that would be faithful
to the nature of life. "The blood-jet," she says in another late
poem, "is poetry" (*A*, p. 82). Poems spring from the same life
consciousness or blood consciousness that exists at the root of
all natural and animal beings. Men, animals, and vegetative life
exist as one in a universe that absorbs them into its blackness
and nothingness; poetry must give expression to the simulta-
neous destructiveness and creativity inherent in existence. In
"The Rabbit Catcher," we see a characteristic formulation of
the ironic interplay of birth and death and of the unity of
animal and human existence. The speaker has walked down a
path lined by spiked gorse bushes toward a hollow with rabbit
traps:

> There was only one place to get to.
> Simmering, perfumed,
> The paths narrowed into the hollow.
> And the snares almost effaced themselves—
> Zeros, shutting on nothing,
>
> Set close, like birth pangs.
>
> [*WT*, p. 35]

Death and birth are ironically equated here. The opening of
the rabbit snares is metaphorically identical to the opening of
the woman's cervix during childbirth. The "zeros" of death
turn out to be the "zeros" of delivery: birth is as painful as
death and brings death into existence. As the poem continues,
we discover that the death prepared for the rabbit is the same
as the death prepared for the human speaker:

> I felt a still busyness, an intent.
> I felt hands round a tea mug, dull, blunt,
> Ringing the white china.

The "hands" are, of course, the hands of the rabbit, and the tea mug and white china are the round snares with their destructive interior. The domestic world of the speaker and the natural world of the rabbit are here one and the same. Death and birth, rabbit and human, play out identical roles in a death process that binds all beings together.

The bondage of human being and organic life to death means, inevitably, a perpetual war against the nonliving universe. Plath sees God as the greatest enemy of man because he either controls, or is, the exterior, inanimate blackness. Against the freezing sky or the darkness of the ocean, the animate self must exert its energies, rushing into destruction so as to affirm its own life. In "Years," for example, God is in his "vacuous black, / Stars stuck all over, bright stupid confetti" (*A*, p. 72). The speaker, in contrast, loves the driving force of her own energy, "The piston in motion," and must race into the future. She wishes to take the same horse ride brilliantly described in "Ariel."

Initiation appears within this context of a deathly, black exterior world and a blood-red animate existence as the means of transcendence to another condition of being. In many of Plath's full-scale initiatory dramas, the self attains a superhuman condition. In "Fever 103°," the speaker becomes the Virgin, ascending to heaven; in "Lady Lazarus," she is a red-haired demon; in "Ariel," an arrow shot to the sun; in "Stopped Dead," a woman who can live off the air; in "Purdah," a fierce lioness. Alternately, she is magically reborn as a baby without the tormented consciousness of the adult, as in "Face Lift," "The Stones," and "Getting There." Or, meditating on her own children, Plath takes on their attributes of freshness and fearlessness in the face of the hostile universe. In a cosmos that is alternately persecutory and inert, the poet summons the courage to face the death forces by undergoing, through the ritual journey, a descent into the blackness. When the descent stops in the midst of the blackness, the poetry seems to mirror the inertness and passivity of nonbeing: poems like "Edge" and

"Words" offer no resistance to the death world. But in much of *Ariel* and *Winter Trees*, Plath rushes into sun, sky, or water to be reborn.

The process of disintegration and renewal that Plath's poems imagine has rarely been dramatized so sensuously and concretely in relation to the physical body. The two poets Plath most resembles in her presentation of ritual processes are D. H. Lawrence and Dylan Thomas, both of whom significantly influenced her work. Both were concerned to find a spiritual value in nonmental life: Lawrence through his search for a "blood consciousness" embedded in animal life; Thomas in his incantatory celebration of the life-and-death movements of the seasons, the body, and nature. Plath found in these poets' exploration of the death-and-rebirth themes a model for an initiatory poetry that strives to come through, as Lawrence might have said, to "a new heaven and new earth." She was, however, less successful than either of these poets in discovering a spiritual home within the universe. Her poems reveal again and again her tremendous violent struggle to gain control of her psyche. Each of Plath's poems portrays in different but parallel settings a momentary ordering of the symbols of life and death. The course of her poetic career, described in the following chapters, follows her growing awareness that the self's encounter with death is the central and all-powerful subject of contemporary poetry.

three

Beginnings

Sylvia Plath's early work differs so greatly from her late poetry both in style and in substance that they would appear to have been written by two different poets. The issues of initiation, death, and rebirth largely govern the poetry from late 1959 until Plath's death in 1963, but her apprentice poems (1950–56) neither hint at these concerns nor suggest the power and psychological dynamics of *Ariel* and *Winter Trees*.[1] The apprentice work includes poems that were written while Plath was at Bradford Senior High School in Wellesley, Massachusetts, and at Smith College in Northampton, Massachusetts. Only the general mood of depression and fear in this body of work anticipates the character of the late poetry. During the apprentice period, Plath found it necessary to stifle feelings and impulses through a spartan devotion to poetic technique: she struggled with poetic diction, with traditional stanza forms, with complex metrical schemes. She had mastered these techniques by the time she left Smith College to go to England in 1956 and had produced a well-contrived, but essentially sterile, body of poems. One of the larger ironies of Plath's career is, in fact, that the sign of her maturation as a poet was her abandonment of the verse techniques she had fought so hard to master from the time she was seventeen years old.

The apprentice work eventually gave way to the greater achievement of *The Colossus*, a volume that contains poems written between 1956 and 1959. In *The Colossus* the formal concerns of the earlier poems are finally combined with a large degree of personal openness. Also, as we shall see, *The Colossus* manipulates the thematic opposition between a negative vision of death and a positive pattern of self-transformation in a way that anticipates the later work. Yet most of this volume is committed to ideals of reticence and self-restraint that conflict with the essentially volatile personal subject matter. Plath discovered toward the end of 1959, which can be taken as the beginning of her later work, the necessity for dramatizing her own situation through a colloquial language and dramatic forms. The discipline demanded by the apprentice poems would help her, but the key development in her growth would be the enactment through poetry of an initiatory process.

Considered as a whole, Plath's early work fits under the category of "academic poetry" of the 1950s. The label "academic" was used by critics and poets in that decade to contrast the traditional poetry, written largely in the universities, with the nonuniversity Beat poetry mainly composed in the San Francisco area. In the early sixties, however, such divisions broke down. Poets like Robert Lowell and James Wright moved away from traditional forms, and, as a result, it seems appropriate to speak of the poetry of the earlier fifties as one of traditional or "closed" forms. The alternative "open" forms have been widely used, though it has not been easy to discuss them with precision.[2]

Plath's development during the late 1950s involved the abandonment of traditional stanza form, traditional rhyme schemes, and a formal, "literary" diction. Philip Levine, another American poet trained in the 1950s, has described the lessons that apprentice poets like Plath learned during this period.[3] In a short memoir, Levine recalls his student days with Yvor Winters, when he was urged to write syllabic poetry like Elizabeth Daryush's, to concentrate on prosodic elements, and to fill up the traditional verse forms in novel ways. The diction of poetry was supposed to be "heightened." Levine comments that his dream during this period was to throw off his training and write a poem in free verse "without employing a heightened vocabulary." He admired Gary Snyder's poems because they were "more readable, more eloquent and looser at the same time, and more consistently in our common American language" than his own work. Like Plath, and around the same time, 1959, Levine "started working toward a different poetry, highly lyrical, heightened with driving, unrelenting rhythm."

Levine's testimony is cited not because he took the same poetic direction as Plath—he did not—but because both turned their backs on the same influences and practices at the same time. Probably the most revealing piece of information about Plath's apprentice poetry relates to her writing technique. She found her "heightened vocabulary" in the Thesaurus: "She wrote her early poems very slow, Thesaurus open on her knee."[4] The earliest examples of her first mode show a bookish, artificial diction that inhibits the flow of image and idea. The traditional forms, as Plath practiced them, demanded a special "poetic" language and a severely logical and linear development of theme.

Among the early, pre-*Colossus* poems, "Go Get the Goodly Squab" stands out as the *reductio ad absurdum* of Plath's devotion to poetic techniques. The idea involved in the poem is never adequately developed. A paraphrase might run: Go ahead and kill slow-witted animals (squab, bears, quail), but do not dare to touch the wild, quick animals (eagles, antelope, mackerel) because nature will punish you for it. Plath gives this strange notion a full-dress, six-stanza treatment. The poem's three even stanzas are in iambic pentameter; its three odd stanzas, in iambic tetrameter. Corresponding lines in the odd stanzas and corresponding lines in the even ones begin with the same word or words; the last lines of the odd stanzas become the first lines of the even stanzas. The rhyme scheme is suitably complex (xaxa abxb cdxc dexe fgfg ghxh), and the heightened diction and alliteration have been thickly laid on. The first two stanzas demonstrate my point:

Go get the goodly squab in the gold-lobed corn
   And pluck the droll-flecked quail where thick they lie,
Go reap the round blue pigeons from roof ridge,
   But let the fast-feathered eagle fly.

Let the fast-feathered eagle fly
And let the sky crack through with thunder;
Hide, hide in the deep nest
Lest the lightning split you asunder.

                                   [*CG*, p. 11]

    Plath's metaphors are conventional exaggerations: the sky "cracking through with thunder" and lightning "splitting" one "asunder." The straining for heightened diction can be felt in the awkward compounds, "droll-flecked," "fast-feathered," and "gold-lobed," which may reflect a reading of Gerard Manley Hopkins. The poem as a whole suggests the negative effects of Plath's concern for technical elements of the traditional mode, especially in the valuation of form over thematic substance. It does demonstrate, though, the attention Plath gave to stanzaic form and poetic structure. This care for language and form became extremely useful later, when she developed her open forms.

    Plath developed a number of ingenious variations on traditional stanza forms in the early poems. In "Second Winter," for example, she develops a Shakespearean sonnet with slant rhymes. It is regularly decasyllabic, but one line is intentionally irregular. After the second quatrain, the sonnet divides decisively, the first eight lines describing the joyous beginning of spring, the last six, the return of winter. The ninth lacks a syllable in order to emphasize the treachery of the winter's reappearance: "Suddenly the traitor climate turns."[5] Prosodic irregularity imitates natural unruliness in this Spenserian piece of wit. Plath worked hard at such technical maneuvers. Her villanelles, like "Doomsday," "To Eva Descending the Stair," and "Mad Girl's Love Song," are technically brilliant, though thematically weak. At an early age she tried a comic variation of ballad material, "Ballade Banale." She wrote a complex variation of terza rima in "Apotheosis," where the first and third lines have four accents, the second line, two, and the rhyme scheme is difficult and original (abb acc add eff egg ehh ijj ikk ill). "Metamorphoses of the Moon" attempts a longer stanza, with six lines per stanza, in which all the lines have five accents except for the third and sixth, which have four. Hardly an early poem of Plath's does not attempt to vary a traditional form.

Plath found models for every aspect of her apprentice poems in the well-known modern British and American poets. Again and again lines and stylistic elements are imitated directly from Wallace Stevens, Dylan Thomas, Robert Lowell, E. E. Cummings, and John Crowe Ransom. "Ballade Banale" is a good example of multiple influence: both Ransom and Cummings are present. The form and diction of the poem derive from Ransom's consciously archaic approach to language and genre. Ransom's balladic tone is behind the opening of "Ballade Banale":

> When I was a maid in the simple town,
>   Red was my hair and white my skin;
> I waltzed on the green in a quilted gown
>   And shattered the hearts of the village men.
>
>   [*CG*, p. 1]

This is an obvious imitation of such Ransom poems as "Eclogue":

> JANE SNEED BEGAN IT: My poor John, alas,
> Ten years ago, pretty it was in a ring
> To run as boys and girls do in the grass—
> At that time leap and hollo and skip and sing
> Came easily to pass.[6]

Cummings's linguistic tricks are also apparent in such lines as "Nights I sailed in my small white bed / In search of someday to change to is."

Ransom also generally influenced Plath toward formality of diction. Although the use of elaborate Latinate language and inversions was common in the forties and fifties, Ransom was probably the most prominent exponent of artifice in poetry. He could write, in an alliterating, precious Latinate idiom:

> Windy gentlemen wreathing a long veranda
> With tongues busy between illicit potations
> Assailing all the acta and / or agenda
> Of previous and / or present administrations:
> Observe that I'm carefully jotting no memoranda
> Lest I seem to identify your wits with your nation's. [7]

The artifice of Plath's early "Dialogue en Route" (1951 or 1952) is modeled on such passages. The dialogue between Eve, the "elevator-girl ace," and Adam, the "arrogant matador," includes this stanza:

> Said Eve: "I wish venomous nematodes
> were bewitched to assiduous lovers,
> each one an inveterate gallant
> with Valentino's crack technical talent
> for recreating down under the covers:
> erotic and elegant episodes." [8]

Plath frequently imitated Dylan Thomas. She used Thomas's image of the poles from "I See the Boys of Summer" ("O see the poles are kissing as they cross"[9]): "we poise on perilous poles that freeze us in / a cross of contradiction" ("Metamorphoses of the Moon" [*L*, p. 9]). In "Lament" she altered Thomas's phrase ("And I am dumb to tell the weather's wind / How time has ticked a heaven round the stars")[10] for her own purposes: ". . . my father / Who scorned the tick of the falling weather" (*CG*, p. 27). The vogue for villanelles in the 1950s, to which Plath contributed, largely stemmed from Thomas's and William Empson's examples.

Robert Lowell's influence can be felt in "Mayflower" (1955), which copies Lowell's interest in colonial history and the Pilgrims in such poems as "Salem," as well as his fondness for alliteration: "So when staunch island stock chose forfeiture / Of the homeland hearth to plough their pilgrim way . . ." (*L*, p. 3). And the Stevens influence is apparent in Plath's version of "Man and Bottle." Stevens had written that the mind is a great poem of winter that "destroys romantic tenements / Of rose and ice";[11] Plath stated that "most exquisite truths are artifice / framed in disciplines of fire and ice" (*L*, p. 8).

Yet Plath's wide-ranging imitations of recognized poets concealed a definite thematic unity in her very early work. The thematic substance of the apprentice poems is completely dominated by visions of despair and death. Plath's first published poem, "Bitter Strawberries," deals with the threat of nuclear annihilation. It anticipates her later projections of disaster. In "Doomsday," Plath imagines the apocalypse: "The idiot bird leaps out and drunken leans / Atop the broken universal clock." The world crumbles: "The painted stages fall apart by scenes / And all the actors halt in mortal shock."[12] But destruction is merely the finale to the world's constant, uncontrolled motion. Movement, change, and instability haunt these early poems: "Clocks cry: stillness is a lie, my dear; / The wheels revolve, the universe keeps running."[13] Amid the ever-changing, and dying, things of the world, Plath's poems call attention to the process of corruption:

> An ill wind is stalking
> while evil stars whir
> and all the gold apples
> go bad to the core.[14]

Yet the recognition of contradiction and conflict in the universe finds expression only within the witty, ironic context of verse written in the 1950s. "Metamorphoses of the Moon" deals with the contradiction between "the fact of doubt" and "the faith of dream," which is a source of despair for the poet. But the language Plath uses eventually undercuts the seriousness of the theme. Innocence, she says, is "a fairy-tale: intelli-

gence / hangs itself on its own rope" (*L*, p. 9). Then, as if
sensing that this last image is too strong, she brings the passage
down to the level of a banal pun: "Either way we choose, the
angry witch / will punish us for saying which is which." Simi-
larly, in "Temper of Time," the tone of the poem is so mixed
that a four-line stanza can begin ominously:

> Black birds of omen
>   now prowl on the bough
>   and the forest is littered . . .

and end comically: "with bills that we owe."[15] In the appren-
tice work obvious expressions of personal unease coexist with
an ironic coyness that attempts to mask them.

In the face of the world's chaos and terror, Plath counsels
her readers, and herself, to maintain an attitude of restraint.
"Admonitions," a villanelle, urges the reader not to be self-
assertive: "Never try to knock on rotten wood, / never try to
know more than you should" (*CG*, p. 15). Intellectual courage
and daring, she warns, will lead only to disappointment, as in
"Metamorphoses of the Moon": ". . . each secret sought / will
prove to be some common parlor fake . . ." (*L*, p. 8). Courage
in the search for knowledge may be dangerous. Plath's Gerd,
the crystal gazer, is punished for her Faustian quest after
knowledge of the future by losing her youthful joyousness.
Her mind becomes "plague-pitted as the moon" (*CG*, p. 18).
Given this world of danger and perpetual disillusionment, it
may be best to risk nothing: "Hide, hide in the warm port /
Lest the water drag you to drown" (*CG*, p. 11).

If the proper response to uncertainty and confusion is self-
restraint, it is also the proper attitude toward love relations,
which are particularly dangerous and unstable. "Ballade Ba-
nale" tells the gloomy story of a girl deserted by her lover, a
juggler. The point of the poem is that the juggler will not allow
the girl to say out loud that she loves him with "her whole
heart." When, unable to restrain herself, she tells him that it is
not just a "glancing" affair, he abandons her immediately.

Once again, restraint is absolutely necessary for emotional stability. In "Dream with Clamdiggers," an autobiographical element is introduced. The speaker dreams that she has returned to her "early sea-town home," evidently a reference to Plath's childhood home at Winthrop, Massachusetts. She regains her lost innocence there, but her happiness offends some clamdiggers at the shore, who are "In wait amid snarled weed and wrack of wave / To trap this wayward girl at her first move of love."[16] Even dreaming of returning to the childhood world of love produces ominous threats to Plath's well-being.

By the time Plath graduated from Smith College in 1955, the elements of the apprentice poetry had been fairly well mastered. Her early themes—the dangerousness of the natural world, the conflict between imagination and reality (faith and doubt), the omnipresence of death—find expression in a terse, alliterative poetry that draws heavily upon the modern poets she had read in high school and in college. "Two Lovers and a Beachcomber by the Real Sea," which won a Glascock poetry prize, illustrates the stage Plath had reached by 1955. It is heavily indebted for its conception to Wallace Stevens's concern with imagination ("The imagination / shuts down its fabled summer house") and to T. S. Eliot's speculations about time:

> . . . what we are
> outlaws all extrapolation
> beyond the interval of now and here. . . .[17]

And it is filled with literary references—to Melville's white whale, to Shakespeare's *The Tempest*, to Eliot's *The Wasteland*. The language of the poem, however, is vivid; and suggests a tension that will dominate *The Colossus*: the desire to reclaim a lost, dead love and the simultaneous recognition that the dead cannot be recovered:

> A lone beachcomber squats among the wreck
> of kaleidoscopic shells

> probing fractured Venus with a stick
> under a tent of taunting gulls.

The "fractured Venus" is an oblique way of expressing the fundamental situation Plath faced throughout her career. A lost, mythologically enlarged past has been shattered; and the poet, alone with her memories, tries to give it new life. Only in *The Colossus* does this theme emerge from below the surface to find a direct, highly charged, and personal expression.

In the period from 1956 through 1959, Plath matured as a poet in the traditional mode. The achievement of *The Colossus and Other Poems* is extraordinary when set beside the raw, imitative attempts of the apprentice work. The carefully made poems of *The Colossus* take up the same obsessions as the earlier ones—nature's violence, restraint and self-control, the fear of death—and yet are as elegant and smooth as the others were forced and harsh. As the reviews at the time of publication made clear, Plath had mastered the formal elements that criticism in the 1950s valued most highly: alliteration and assonance, difficult stanza forms, and a highly charged diction.[18]

The focus of the apprentice poems had been diffuse: Plath was obviously experimenting with ideas and personal experience whose shape has not yet been clarified through poetry. But by the time *The Colossus* was written, she had come upon the dynamic contrast that determines the form of her later poetry. In the *Colossus* poems, she sees the world as split between two warring principles, death and life, that limit her desires and control the possibilities of existence in general. Specifically, she divides the visible universe into those objects or people that aid the self in its struggle to survive and those that attack and persecute the individual or race. The death force in the universe embodies itself in five separate forms, each of which provides the subject for different poems. The poems about death in *The Colossus* can be separated into those that mainly deal with animals, with nature, with the family, with human or animal corpses, and with women. Although these poems superficially appear to speak about different areas of experiences, they all share a common imagery that allows Plath to treat death's omnipresent figure. Contrastingly, the poems on the affirmative and self-transformative aspects of existence focus on birth and rebirth, on art, and on vision. Several poems, like "Medallion" and "Blue Moles," begin by concentrating on death and then move toward affirmation and transformation; but the mood of the volume is defined by the obsession with death and dead objects.

By 1959 she had come to see her subject as the conflict between death and rebirth. The organization of the poems in the volume exemplifies this informing thematic opposition: the first poem in *The Colossus*, "The Manor Garden" (1959), addresses an unborn child, whose future existence is over-shadowed by omens of natural disaster; the last, "Poem for a Birthday" (1959), imagines a completely new body for the speaker, who has thrown off her old, dead self.[19] Since both these poems were written at the very end of the 1956–59 period covered by the volume, it is safe to assume that Plath deliberately gave *The Colossus* a thematic frame, beginning the volume with the prospect of a real birth and ending it with a symbolic rebirth.

The title of the volume further supports this notion. The title poem, "The Colossus," is about rebirth, or, rather, about the hoped-for rebirth of the dead father. By choosing the colossus image as her organizing metaphor for the volume, Plath concentrates her readers' attention upon the dead and upon her attempt to bring them back to life. As the last poem of the volume, "The Stones," shows, this desire for rebirth eventually finds expression in the poet's enactment of a drama of rebirth.

A fine example of Plath's treatment of the theme of death in *The Colossus* is "Mushrooms" (1959), a poem that sees mush-rooms as a form of menacing animal life. "Mushrooms" fanta-sizes about natural life by projecting a human consciousness

onto alien existence and then rendering that "mind" through a
brilliant poetic technique. It is representative of the poems that
deal with animals and nature.

> Overnight, very
>
> Whitely, discreetly,
> Very quietly
>
> Our toes, our noses
> Take hold on the loam,
> Acquire the air.
>
> Nobody sees us,
> Stops us, betrays us;
> The small grains make room.
>
> Soft fists insist on
> Heaving the needles,
> The leafy bedding,
>
> Even the paving.
> Our hammers, our rams,
> Earless and eyeless,
>
> Perfectly voiceless,
> Widen the crannies,
> Shoulder through holes. We
>
> Diet on water,
> On crumbs of shadow,
> Bland-mannered, asking
>
> Little or nothing.
> So many of us!
> So many of us!
>
> We are shelves, we are
> Tables, we are meek,
> We are edible,

Nudgers and shovers
In spite of ourselves.
Our kind multiplies:

We shall by morning
Inherit the earth.
Our foot's in the door.

[C, pp. 37–38]

The difference between "Mushrooms" and the earlier ap-
prentice work lies in the specific attention Plath has paid, first,
to the visual details of the fantasized animallike mushrooms
and, second, to the aural qualities of her language. Visually,
the poem gives us a race of mobile mushrooms: animal or
human forms are projected onto these small natural shapes.
The mushrooms' roots become toes; their stems, noses; their
caps, fists. These creatures quietly and "whitely" push through
the forest floor like an army of soldiers. Here Plath's visual
imagination anticipates the later brilliant images of *Ariel*: "bed-
ding" and "paving" are "heaved" up; the "shelves" and "tables"
of the caps cover the once-pastoral forest area. With an ironic
nod to Tennyson's "flower in the crannied wall," Plath finds
sinister "crannies" through which the mushrooms "shoulder"
their way into the light. As in the later poem "Elm," Plath
makes nature speak in its own voice out of a consciousness that
is animate through and through.

The visual specificity of the poem goes along with a remark-
able attention to sound repetition. The rhyme of *night* and
white in the first two lines and the assonance on the *e*-sound
("very," "whitely," "discreetly," "quietly") are brilliant touches.
Assonance and rhyme work beautifully throughout the poem.
Line 4 has internal rhyme; line 5, assonance; and line 6,
alliteration. In the third stanza, eight of the twelve words
alliterate on *s*; and line 10 alliterates five different *s*'s and two
f's. Lines 10 through 13 play on the *e*-sound five times.

In addition, the metrical scheme is demanding and well
handled. The five-syllable lines and three-line stanzas allow

the poem to flow evenly and gracefully, as the stanza forms of "Go Get the Goodly Squab" had not. The word choice is also appropriate to the poem's speaker, the humanoid mushroom. "Acquire the air" suggests the threatened appropriation of the world by the mushrooms; "heaving the needles" conjures up the gigantic effort on the part of the small; and "soft fists" marvelously condenses the aggressiveness of the weak into two monosyllables. The reference in the final stanza to the meek's inheritance of the earth contrasts ironically with the mushrooms' violent, nonreligious method of "inheritance." The final colloquial, jarring phrase, "Our foot's in the door," is perhaps the only blemish in the texture of the poem.

"Mushrooms" is characteristic of the fine, brilliant technique demonstrated throughout *The Colossus*. Plath shows her mastery of both syllabic and accentual lines. The sound effects are often superb; and the several types of poems—narrative, lyric, and dramatic monologue—give the book an unusual range. Lapses in diction only occasionally damage the overall effect of the poems: her besetting fault is a tendency to use uninspired, tired colloquialisms. Not until "Fever 103°" and "Ariel" is she completely in command of a colloquial idiom.

But the dominant fault in these poems is not in the technical application of poetic method, but in the suitability of the poetic mode to Plath's themes. The true subject matter of these poems lies buried within them, as sometimes one painting is hidden under the surface of another. In "Mushrooms," for example, the originating idea—a world takeover by the small mushrooms—never receives a multidimensional development. Instead, Plath caricatures human reality by projecting only aggressiveness onto the natural object, the mushrooms. Once she has narrowed the subject this far, and the human agent has been excluded from the poem, the thematic progression—from weak to strong, from fungus to conqueror of the world—can only be linear and predictable. She has too greatly restricted the range of possible meanings and references. The poem suffers from a limitation imposed upon its subject matter.

The same criticism can be made of the other poems in *The Colossus* that focus on either animals or nature. Plath found in both these topics a means of simplifying and focusing her obsessions with death and danger. In "The Bull of Bendylaw" (1956), a mythical bull makes the sea rise, destroys the kingdom of Bendylaw, and establishes himself as master of the land after deposing the king and queen. "Sow" (1956) portrays a gigantic sow, who is contained within a farmyard. This sow threatens to "swill / The seven troughed seas and every earth-quaking continent" (*C*, p. 11). The comic or light tone of these poems belies Plath's very deep concern with the enlarged figures of nature and with the hostility the natural world may show to men. The syllabics of "Sow" and "Mushrooms" and the balladic lilt of "The Bull of Bendylaw" restrain emotional material that, in another context, erupt in the charged images of dangerous animals in "Totem" or in the fearful bees in *Ariel*.

Infrequently, animals, like the frogs in the riddle-poem "Frog Autumn" (1957), will be victims of nature rather than persecutors of others; but Plath's main sense of other animate beings is of their potential to become wild and dangerous. Animals often bring death to the self and to the race, which then appears vulnerable and unprotected. Plath was evidently obsessed with such a prospect. In *The Colossus* she writes about a giant sow, a gigantic bull, wolves, wasps, and sharks, dangerous mushrooms, owls, foxes, frogs, spiders, crabs, and bees. These animals form a bestiary whose main symbolic purpose is to embody the life-and-death struggle of the poet herself.

Similarly, the poems on nature generally speak of the non-human environment, landscape or seascape, as hostile to all human desire and intention. In fact, nature's indifference or resistance to human desire pervades almost all of the poems in *The Colossus*, even those dealing with the family or with women. Plath typically locates her poems near the ocean, which is destructive and rough (Plath grew up near the Atlantic Ocean), or in a rocky landscape that gives little or no response to the poet's desire for relationship. As a result, the characteristic imagery of the nature poems pervades her poetry. She continually returns to images of stone and water: stone resists the poet's attempt to communicate with nature; water threatens the security of the land and human habitation. The natural world as a whole is thus metaphorically the field of battle for the poet's life-and-death struggle.

Perhaps the clearest account of the relationship between self and nature in *The Colossus* appears in the first of the poems about nature, "Hardcastle Crags" (1956), which describes a rocky landscape. The poem demonstrates that the natural world can hurt the poet even when she merely wants to walk about and observe it. Perception itself, according to "Hardcastle Crags," can endanger the sense of a stable, strong selfhood. A woman walks in the valley of the Pennines in West York and records her experiences of the world around her— the town, the grass, the moon, the wind, the hills. Nature, she says, "could break / Her down to mere quartz grit" (*C*, p. 16). The dominant images of the poem all suggest a similar fear of hard objects: flint, steel, stone, iron, and granite. The word *stone* appears no less than seven times: the "stone-built town," the "pastures bordered by black stone set / On black stone," the sheep drowsing "stoneward," the "weight / Of stones and hills of stones," and the "stony light" of the night world. The girl walks amid this nonhuman scene in a "blank mood," that is, in a state without the comforting shapes of dreams or the companionship of human beings. "Blankness," in Plath's lexicon, is the perceptual state that occurs when the world is seen as hard stone. Simply to perceive these items of the natural world is to be weighted down by them, to feel the oppressiveness of the inhuman and the alien:

> All the night gave her, in return
> For the paltry gift of her bulk and the beat
> Of her heart was the humped indifferent iron
> Of its hills, and its pastures bordered by black stone set
> On black stone.

[C, p. 15]

The girl feels reduced in size and importance in relation to an "indifferent" nature; she begins to fear that her human flame cannot survive in the "antique world" of the landscape. Frightened of losing her self totally, she turns back from the landscape to the town from which she came. The stone, the hills, and the moon, perceived in their otherness and externality, seem capable of breaking down and destroying the human body. In Plath's world, landscape is as threatening as any wild beast or giant sow because it may turn the barely surviving human self into stone or mineral. No more antithetical attitude to Wordsworth's adoration of the natural can be imagined! Plath, who has often been called a Romantic poet, is the inversion of Wordsworth: she writes obsessively about nature not because of her love for it but because of her overwhelming terror in the face of it.

The hardness and stoniness of the landscape carries over to the seascape "Departure" (1956), the next nature poem in *The Colossus*. This panorama of the Spanish seashore, which Plath visited with her husband in the summer of 1956, emphasizes the brutality of the sea and the poverty of nature:

> Retrospect shall not soften such penury—
> Sun's brass, the moon's steely patinas,
> The leaden slag of the world—
> But always expose
>
> The scraggy rock spit shielding the town's blue bay
> Against which the brunt of outer sea
> Beats, is brutal endlessly.

> [*C*, p. 18]

Brass, steel, lead, rock: the imagery of unyielding hardness applies to both the land and the heavens. The sun and the moon are hostile to human life; the sea violently attacks the earth. The human agents in the poem receive only two brief mentions: "The money's run out"; "Ungifted, ungrieved, our leavetaking." The point of the poem lies not in the couple's action or response *to* nature, but in the poet's longing for a response *from* nature. What is desired, however, never comes to pass; and the final sense of this, and of many poems in *The Colossus*, is of an absent response. As becomes clear from the rest of the volume, Plath not only obtains no response from nature, but none from the dead father and dead grandmother, from the dead animals, or from the objects that have been left behind as reminders (statues, corpses) of once-existent beings.

The other nature poems in *The Colossus* enforce a similar sense of bleakness and absence, with the exception of "Watercolour of Grantchester Meadows," which is for the most part a purely pastoral account of the natural world. Here the landscape is benign. The poem deliberately portrays the beautiful animal life around the Granta River near Cambridge, England, where Plath attended university for two years. Sheep, thumb-sized birds, cygnets, and happy cows dot the scene as black-gowned students from Cambridge enjoy themselves. For once in *The Colossus*, Plath seems to be writing about the "benign / Arcadian green" (p. 41), one of the central motifs of Western nature poetry. But pastoralism is definitively negated by the poem's last line. The only reason the students can bask in this Arcadian green is because they are ignorant of the predatory scene that will occur out of their sight; near them in the "mild air, / The owl shall stoop from his turret, the rat cry out."

The direct confrontation of a pastoral with a naturalistic vision is an interesting development in the series of nature poems in *The Colossus*. The opposition between Edenic innocence and natural violence parallels another pattern that occurs throughout Plath's work: the polarity of a dreamlike happiness, usually found underwater or in sleep, and the waking state of pain and disillusionment. This polarity characterizes "The Ghost's Leavetaking" (1957–58), originally entitled "Departure of the Ghost." The ghost of the title is the spirit of the dream world, "ghost of our mother and father, ghost of us, / And ghost of our dreams' children" (p. 43). The lost childhood of the poet springs alive during sleep with its nursery rhymes ("The Cow Jumped over the Moon") and its fantastic possibilities. Reality, however, is characterized by a "no-color void." Objects like chairs and bureaus are momentarily suffused in a dream aura when we wake up, but they quickly lose their ghostliness in the light of day. Like nature's "blankness," reality's void is always waiting to ensnare the solitary self, either through its threatening indifference or its actual hostility. Whether nature momentarily looks like paradise or sleep temporarily looks like heaven, these appearances of peacefulness are deceptive: what really awaits us is suffering and blankness.

This view of nature as alternately hostile or indifferent characterizes such poems as "A Winter Ship," "Suicide off Egg Rock," "Mussel Hunter at Rock Harbor," "Man in Black," "Snakecharmer," and "The Hermit at Outermost House." In "A Winter Ship" (1959), the speaker goes to the wharves to see a brilliant sunrise, but her expectations are spoiled: "We wanted to see the sun come up / And are met, instead, by this iceribbed ship" (*C*, p. 45). The sea is dirty; the warehouses, derricks, and bridges are worn out and rickety. The imagery represents nature as degenerate, a place of waste created by the machinery that man has built. A gull has a "jacket of ashes," and smells of "dead cod and tar" mingle. The ship is so run-down that Plath speaks of it as an "icy albatross," alluding to Coleridge's "The Rime of the Ancient Mariner." But even in its icy condition, the ship will continue to suffer from the sun and waves. "A Winter Ship" perfectly recapitulates the situation, images, and theme of the group of poems dealing with landscapes and seascapes: a human being or man-made object attacked by, or threatened by attack from, natural forces— stones, sea, or sun.

In "Suicide off Egg-Rock" (1958–59), the connection between death and the sea receives a more complex treatment. This third-person narration of a young man's suicide stresses the deadness of the industrial landscape near the Massachusetts shore, with its gas tanks and factory stacks, as well as the young man's corresponding inner feelings of deadness. He has come to feel as if he himself were made out of steel or metal:

"His body beached with the sea's garbage, / A machine to breathe and beat forever" (*C*, p. 35). Identity itself, the "I am, I am, I am," becomes unbearably meaningless and repetitious. Like the girl in "Hardcastle Crags," he suffers from a perceptual blankness, the sense that the scene before him is without solidity and substance: "Everything glittered like blank paper" (p. 36). The only solid identity is, once again, rock, Egg Rock; but rock gains its solidity at the price of nonresponsiveness. This powerful poem, with its echoes of Robert Lowell's harsh alliterative language ("the spindrift / Ravelled wind-ripped from the crest of the wave"), precisely captures the alternatives that the natural world and the family leave open for Plath: unremitting attack from the hard, meaningless, repetitious force of nature or descent into the water of forgetfulness, "The forgetful surf creaming on those ledges." It suggests that water may conceal a double emotional meaning—of both fear and escape from fear—below its surface.

To turn from the poems on animals and nature to those dealing with the family in *The Colossus* is to see the struggle between weak and strong, human and nonhuman, intensified and complicated. The death of family members exposes the brutality of death more intensely and personally than does the threat of animals or nature; but it also, simultaneously, makes it more imperative for the poet to discover a means of escape from annihilation. In "Point Shirley," "The Colossus," "All the Dead Dears," "The Disquieting Muses," "The Beekeeper's Daughter," and "Full Fathom Five," death is seen as both the enemy of everything that the self loves and the ultimate escape from the life of pain. In these poems the poet's father, mother, and grandmother are the explicit subjects, and thus the material becomes more personally charged than in the series on nature and animals. The family provides Plath with her most ambiguous examples of death's power to undo the entire web of loving relations with the world. In Plath's imagination love and death often become confused and entangled. It is often unclear, for example, if the speaker loves her dead father or if, in fact, she ever loved him. The father becomes the central object of conflict, for he is the focus of widely divergent opinions: that he still lives under the sea ("Full Fathom Five") or that he cannot be said to live anymore ("The Colossus").

In representing her conflicting feelings toward the death of loved parents or grandparents, Plath turns to the same complex of images that she uses in her poems about nature. In fact, it is often impossible to distinguish between her consideration of the natural environment and her consideration of the family members, so connected in her imagination are the places and images associated with the father, mother, and grandparents. For example, in "Point Shirley" the grandmother's home in Winthrop, Massachusetts, *becomes* the grandmother. The dead relative now literally *is* the purple egg-stones that she has embedded in the "stucco sockets" of the old sea-battered house. The vicious winds and tides represent, then, the death that has taken the grandmother away from the poet: nature and death are really one and the same agency. "Steadily," Plath says, "the sea / Eats at Point Shirley" (C, p. 25). The "sluttish, rutted sea" ravages the past and the grandmother's house, leaving the poet with only a desperate hope:

> I would get from these dry-papped stones
> The milk your love instilled in them.
> The black ducks dive.
> And though your graciousness might stream,
> And I contrive,
> Grandmother, stones are nothing of home
> To that spumiest dove.
> Against both bar and tower the black sea runs.
>
> [C, pp. 25–26]

The poet wants to convert the round egg-stones into breasts and to resurrect the lost grandmother's body. But milk will not come from stone; stone will not be humanized; nature will not become a maternal figure. "Point Shirley," like the nature poems, ends with a resigned and bitter realization that lost love and lost relationship are irrecuperable. The dead family, embodied for Plath in the battered house beside a violent Atlantic Ocean where she grew up, will not be reborn.

A similar development of the family motif occurs in "The Colossus," with an identical imagistic play on the hardness of stone and lost love. Plath imagines that the Colossus, which once dominated the harbor at Rhodes, is her father's dead body, now lying broken in pieces on a hillside. The father's "ancient" power and size have been destroyed through time. The Colossus image embodies both the poet's fear of the stonelike, resistant force of the patriarch and her admiration for the colossal power that her father once possessed. The broken statue indicates, as "Point Shirley" did, that the dead man cannot be recovered through piecing him, or the poet's memories of him, together again, although the poet continues to gaze in fear and love at him.

Plath had used the Colossus image once before, in an apprentice poem called "Letter to a Purist" (1956), without identifying the statue with her father and without imagining that the statue had been broken into pieces:

> That grandiose colossus who
> Stood astride
> The envious assaults of the sea
> (Essaying, wave by wave,
> Tide by tide,
> To undo him perpetually),
> Has nothing on you,
> O my love,
>
> O my great idiot, who
> With one foot
> Caught (as it were) in the muck-trap
> Of skin and bone,
> Dithers with the other way out
> In preposterous provinces of the mad cap

> Cloud-cuckoo,
> Agawp at the impeccable moon.[20]

In the much superior poem in *The Colossus*, Plath successfully uses the statue as a symbol for the father's vanished power. Instead of the awkward and arch language of the earlier poem ("essaying," "agawp," "as it were"), she finds a more colloquial, though still somewhat stilted, language with which to address her father:

> I shall never get you put together entirely,
> Pieced, glued, and properly jointed.
> Mule bray, pig-grunt and bawdy cackles
> Proceed from your great lips.
> It's worse than a barnyard.

> [*C*, p. 20]

While the first lines still imitate a literary source, Dylan Thomas's elegy for Ann Jones ("After the funeral, mule praises, brays"[21]), the poem goes on to discover its own language of praise and contempt for the father. The central metaphor is ingeniously varied, as in the comparison of the eyes of the statue to "bald white tumuli" or in the conversion of the tongue into a pillar. By sticking to the fantasized situation—a young daughter's archaeological reconstruction of the father-statue—Plath gives a surrealistic quality to the metaphor. We seem to be at a halfway point between the psychic obsessions of an interior drama and the public concerns of the archaeologist. The poem is still split, though, between two objectives: the expression of a vitriolic contempt for the abandoning father and a rigid pride in his all-powerful, paternal authority. "The Colossus" is halfway to "Daddy" from the earlier "Letter to a Purist."

In "Full Fathom Five," by contrast, the father's image is untarnished, and the syllabics easily cover the abyss separating father from daughter. In this fantasy of paternal rebirth, the father lives in the water that Shakespeare, in *The Tempest*, had imagined as the water of transformation. Rather than being embedded forever in the fixed form of statuary, the father is carried by the tides before the daughter's ceaselessly loving eyes:

> Miles long
>
> Extend the radial sheaves
> Of your spread hair, in which wrinkling skeins
> Knotted, caught, survives
>
> The old myth of origins
> Unimaginable.
>
> [*C*, p. 46]

In further contrast to "The Colossus" or "Point Shirley," "Full Fathom Five" presents water not as a force that has destroyed the family member once and for all, but as the living environment for the dead. Unable to distinguish clearly between the dead father's shape in the imagination, preserved forever amid the seascapes of the Massachusetts shore, and the actuality of death itself, the poet symbolically wishes for her own death by saying: "Father, this air is murderous. / I would breathe water" (*C*, p. 48). To breathe water is, of course, to enter the father's underwater world; but it is also to lose one's life, to commit suicide. As in "Suicide off Egg Rock," Plath holds out the possibility that the self may be "forgotten" in the water and there rediscover its lost world of happiness.

The paradox of Plath's relation to death lies in this contradictory use of the images of water and ocean. Whereas the poems of nature typically view the sea as a negative force, a number of significant poems, including "Full Fathom Five," "Suicide off Egg Rock," and "Lorelei" (1957–58), convert what is feared, personal annihilation, into a means of escape from death. In this procedure they anticipate the characteristic initiatory methods of *Ariel* and *Winter Trees*. In "Lorelei," for example, Plath makes use of the legend of the Germanic sirens who lured sailors to their deaths on the Rhine and of the undersea expeditions of Jacques Cousteau.[22] As an invocation

to the sirens, "Those great goddesses of peace," to take the
speaker down to the beautiful world below, the poem presents
a death-wish, just as "Full Fathom Five" presented a death-
wish in relation to the paternal figure. Paradoxically, the im-
ages of stone and water in "Lorelei" symbolize a desired state
of being, since death by water now seems attractive to the self.
The sirens have "hair heavier / Than sculpted marble" (*C*,
p. 22); and the poet asks the stone to carry her down to the
watery world of peace: "Stone, stone ferry me down there"
(p. 23).

If it appears curious that stone and water should be valued
in such a contradictory fashion in Plath's poems, it is because
she actually shifts between two opposed relationships with
the world. In the nature poems, like "Hardcastle Crags" and
"Mushrooms," and in the family poems, like "The Colossus,"
the self is distant and alien from the external universe. Objects
and people are "hard," indifferent, objectified. In such poems
as "Lorelei" and "Full Fathom Five," however, the self can
imagine merger and identification with nature and other people.
We might say that, in the first case, nature is identified with
the father as hardened and set in death, and, in the second
case, with the father and mother as fluid, changing beings.
The two relations to the external world, objectification and
identification, are embodied in the same natural images, stone,
water, sun, and moon; but the emotional charge of these
images changes with the mode of relation. At one moment, the
sun is a destructive force; in the next, it is a purifying and life-
giving agent.

Plath thus characteristically presents opposite reactions to
the same set of objects, people, or landscapes in different
poems. Behind this practice of reversing the symbolic charge
of a given image lies her polarized view of reality: her alternat-
ing attraction to and repulsion from the natural world; her love
of and hatred for the family; and, as I shall show, her desire for
and fear of death.

The objectification of others and of nature can be seen in a poem that deals alternately with nature, with the family, and with the bodies of the dead, "All the Dead Dears" (1956). The initial focus of the poem is a number of skeletons on display in a museum; but "All the Dead Dears" rapidly becomes a meditation on the relation between the poet and her family. The setting is the Archaeological Museum in Cambridge, England, where the ancient skeleton of a woman lies in a case along with the skeletons of a mouse and a shrew. The archaeological motif immediately joins the poem to "The Colossus," with its interest in the broken statuary of the father's image, and the images of crushing and pounding link the poem to "Hardcastle Crags." "Stars," according to "All the Dead Dears," are "grinding, crumb by crumb, / Our own grist down to its bony face" (*C*, p. 29). This gruesome sense of cosmic oppression has its parallel in familial oppression. Rather than being protectors of the self, the family members now seem to drag the poet into the watery underworld of the dead (experienced as an unwanted world), where they exist. "The dead dears" of the title are "outlaws," who make an appearance at all family gatherings—dead father, dead great-grandfather, dead mother and grandmother. In a pun on "wedlock," the poet sees herself "deadlocked" with the family, while the newborn rock in their cradles.

In "All the Dead Dears," then, Plath completely reverses the sense of the family as a loving group whom death destroys and whom she wishes to recover either from their frozen, entombed state or from their watery graves. Instead, the family is identified with the hard, crushing world of nature and death outside her that threatens her selfhood and her continued existence. The reason for this antithetical view of the family is suggested by the three stanzas that appeared in an earlier version of the poem, when it was submitted as part of Plath's English Tripos at Cambridge.[23] Stanzas 4, 5, and part of stanza 8 of this version were eventually dropped, possibly because Plath found that they unbalanced the original poem. Since stanzas 4 and 5 of the original version concentrate so intensively on the dead father and his beekeeping, she may have felt that they were misplaced in a poem about all the dead family members.[24] Whatever the actual reason, the deleted stanzas imply that the speaker has been crushed by her love for the dead family members: "Luck's hard which falls to love / Such long gone darlings." If she could forget her love and their death, she might live a happier life, since her family constantly reminds her of her own death. But such an escape is impossible. She recognizes that by loving the dead, she is imprisoned in a dream of regained childhood that can never be realized. The family becomes a persecutory agency representing the cosmic forces of death and cyclical destruction.

The persecutory force of the past reappears in "The Disquieting Muses" (1958), which again blames the family for leaving the poet in a world of stone. The poem is split between two opposite attitudes: joy at having successfully banished the mother's image and despair at having failed to destroy the Three Disquieting Muses, who are the symbolic substitutes for the mother's negative image.[25] Like so many threatening and dangerous objects in *The Colossus*, the muses are made of stone, and they haunt the poet wherever she goes:

> Day now, night now, at head, side, feet,
> They stand their vigil in gowns of stone,
> Faces blank as the day I was born,
> Their shadows long in the setting sun
> That never brightens or goes down.

> [*C*, p. 60]

The daughter blames her mother for not having protected her from the evil influence of the muses, who are actually more furies than poetic spirits. Although Plath commemorates the day she rejected her mother, she feels trapped by the hostile gaze of the muses, who substitute for the mother; their stoniness, blankness, and unchangingness associate them with those aspects of the natural world and of death that Plath fears most. In one sense, "The Disquieting Muses" accounts for the prevalence of menace and fatality in *The Colossus*, since it attributes this mood to the persistence into adult life of childhood fantasies. Once again, the attitude of fatality and resignation in the face of the universe is Plath's only possible response.

Plath's highly ambivalent attitude toward the family also characterizes her view of women. Like the family members, women represent ambiguous beings: they are at once alive and dead, loved and hated. This duality in the poems on women is generally expressed through the opposition of fertility and sterility. In "Two Sisters of Persephone" (1957), "Spinster" (1956), "Moonrise" (1959), "Medea" (1956), and "Metaphors" (1959), Plath sees women as intensely vulnerable to attack. They can defend themselves either by becoming sterile, virginal creatures or by giving birth to children and becoming mothers. The paradigm for women in Plath's poems, then, opposes death and life in the most absolute of terms. The body either dies because it does not bear children or it lives because it has become fertile.

This contrast produces a schematic design in the poems on women. For example, one of the sisters in "Two Sisters of Persephone" is virginal and dies prematurely; the other becomes a mother and thrives. The speaker in "Spinster" identifies men with nature's assaults against human beings (the "mutinous weather") and protects herself with "barricades of barb and cheek." She lives unhappily. Medea is portrayed as similarly condemned to a living death because she destroys her own children. In contrast, the exuberant speaker of the riddle-poem "Metaphors," written in nine lines of nine syllables each, compares herself to animal life, to fruit, and to housing; and the speaker in "Moonrise" tentatively expresses faith in the process of birth, after many images of death and pain: "The white stomach may ripen yet" (*C*, p. 65).

The unifying element in these poems, though, lies in the common biological fate facing the women, since each of them may die: spinsterhood is living death; motherhood may end in death or suffering because of childbirth. The best of the poems on women in *The Colossus*, "Moonrise," exemplifies this conflict. It employs a clipped, colloquial speech, in triadic stanza form, and opposes images of redness, which represent the forces of growth, to images of whiteness, which represent forces of death. As the speaker sits in a field, she compares the pervasive fact of death, the corpses underground, and the memories of her dead father with her own prospective delivery. Balancing the vision of cyclical and generational destruction against her own sense of fertility, she is unable to avoid an intense fear of death. But "Moonrise" releases, as only a few of *The Colossus* poems do, personal images of death in a dynamic way as Plath works toward a resolution of the death-fear, allowing her to see her experience as part of a recurrent pattern in nature.

The two conflicting modes of perceiving nature, animals, the family, and women as either the frightening dead or the vital living, as objectified enemies or as internalized friends, culminates in a series of poems that directly confront the face of death. In this strange group of poems on corpses, Plath observes a dissected body ("Two Views of a Cadaver Room"), two dead moles ("Blue Moles"), a dead fiddler crab ("Mussel Hunter at Rock Harbor"), a dead snake ("Medallion"), and the "corpse" of a "dead" building ("The Burnt-Out Spa"). As a group, these poems again suggest the doubleness of Plath's vision: they alternately keep the dead, frightening bodies at a distance and attempt to humanize them either through direct identification or through the transformative process of art.

"Blue Moles" is characteristic of Plath's dual relationship with the dead. It is divided into two parts. The first section objectifies the dead moles, whereas the second section involves identification with them. The qualities Plath ascribes to these dead animals mirror the qualities she assigns to hostile nature, to dead family members, and to victimized animals—that is, to all objects that are outside the self. The moles are white ("their white hands / Uplifted, . . ."), which is, in other poems, the "no-color" or void color of death. In "Moonrise" she writes: "Death whitens in the egg and out of it. . . . / White: it is a complexion of the mind." (*C*, p. 65). They are "neutral," which is to say, without feeling, "blank"; and they are stonelike: "The moles look neutral as the stones." They are leathery, "Shapeless as flung gloves," which links them to dead, processed animal skins. Finally, they remind her of a dead family: ". . . their white hands / Uplifted, stiffen in a family pose."

The qualities ascribed to the moles—stiffness, leatheriness, stoniness, neutrality, and whiteness—belong to an objectified nature, a dead family, a petrified world. Against such a "hard" world, which is utterly other to the speaker, the second section of the poem places the soft underworld of the moles, into which the poet enters. The second section is less harsh and more lyrical than the first:

> Nightly the battle-shouts start up
> In the ear of the veteran, and again
> I enter the soft pelt of the mole.
> Light's death to them: they shrivel in it.
> They move through their mute rooms while I sleep,
> Palming the earth aside, grubbers
> After the fat children of root and rock.
>
> [*C*, p. 50]

This marvelous passage suggests the liberation Plath achieves through identification: she goes inside the mole's skin and finds a self that is akin to animal life. In the darkness of the earth an endless search for food takes place without anxiety or fear. By becoming one with the moles, she abandons her human identity, which had been one of fearfulness and vulnerability, and takes on the characteristics of the fetus, the animal, and the dreamer, who are ensconced safely in the womb of the mother, of sleep, and of the earth. It is as if the earth has become a body for the moles and, consequently, for the poet: "Outsize hands prepare a path, / They go before: opening the veins, . . ." Absorption, which attracted the poet to the waters of the Lorelei, draws her down into the darkness of the animal world.

The dual view of nature, self, and death in "Blue Moles" is

repeated in "Two Views of a Cadaver Room," though with a considerable difference in its second section. Again, the poem is split into two parts. The first section is a third-person objective narration of a woman's visit to a dissecting room, a visit that Plath also describes in *The Bell Jar*.[26] Objectification again produces a series of disturbing perceptions. The four corpses in the room seem to the woman to be made of animal flesh ("burnt turkey"); the skin and bones of one head are "skull plates and old leather" (*C*, p. 5). These transformations of the body reflect the poet's disgust at the sight of death: in the first case, the corpse is nothing but inedible meat; in the second, it is worthless old leather. A different note creeps into the account, though, as the speaker describes the fetuses em-balmed in jars along the wall: "In their jars the snail-nosed babies moon and glow."[27] A kind of perverse attraction to the enclosed babies appears here, as if enclosure in a protected area, even though it involves death, may be desirable.

In the second part of the poem, Plath moves away from the objectification of the dead. As in "Blue Moles," she switches to a more sympathetic account of the individual self, although here the identification is limited and less effective. She now transforms death through aesthetic means. In the second part, Plath uses the same method W. H. Auden had used in "Musée des Beaux Arts": thematic development through a commentary on a painting by Brueghel. Auden had described "The Fall of Icarus"; Plath shows us "The Triumph of Death." The art historian Piero Bianconi describes Brueghel's "Triumph of Death" in this way: "Death . . . triumph[s] over all sorts of conditions given. In the foreground are certain carefully de-fined examples; the King, the Cardinal, the Housewife with her distaff and her baby . . . ; a fashionable young couple . . . on the extreme right are still at their music-making, but the young man looks haunted, and a skeleton is accompanying them on a viol."[28] Plath concentrates on this couple, "blind to the carrion army," and finds in their momentary preservation a stay against death. "Blind love" counterbalances, for an instant, the progress of destruction. But the poem, whose "positive" moment hardly counterbalances its horrific first section, does not really overcome the sense of a death world that has erased all feeling and human sensitivity.

Two other poems about corpses also suggest an escape from objectification through aesthetic transformation. In "Medallion" (1959) and "Mussel Hunter at Rock Harbor" (1959), dead bodies are transformed into aesthetic objects; and this conversion of the frightening and disfigured into the beautiful lessens the pain of confronting death. The subject of "Medallion" is, like that of "Blue Moles," a dead animal. The terza rima descripton of the dead snake transforms it into an ornamental object: the snake's scales are jewels; the snake itself becomes "Pure death's metal" (*C*, p. 62). The title suggests that the poem can make death into an ornament, although this can occur only through overlooking the degenerating organic state of the body. All the negative qualities that Plath normally assigns to the dead—hardness, blankness, and inertness—thus recur in the poem; but they are superseded by a kind of gleeful aesthetic control exercised over the frightening emotional realities of the snake.

Similarly, though less intensely, "Mussel Hunter at Rock Harbor" involves the characteristic negative rehearsal of the deathlike qualities of the dead crab. The speaker obviously loves the Massachusetts shore, where she has gone to dig for mussels, but she feels shut out from the natural world. The aggressiveness of the sea life disturbs her; the crabs' claws are "grimly / Borne, for a use beyond my / Guessing of it" (*C*, p. 70). But by the end of the poem she has converted the feared object into an artifact:

> The crab-face, etched and set there,
>
> Grimaced as skulls grimace: it
> Had an Oriental look,
> A samurai death mask done

On a tiger tooth, less for
Art's sake than God's.

[p. 72]

The crab turns into a "relic," as the snake, in "Medallion," had become a "jewel." Instead of identifying with these animals, which is the method of "Blue Moles" and of the later poetry, Plath turns them into religious or aesthetic objects.

The most comprehensive poem dealing with the dead body is "The Burnt-Out Spa," which can be taken as Plath's summation of the various motifs I have been describing. The poet speaks of a burnt-out building as if it were the body of an "old beast"; she sees her role in inspecting the building as an "archaeologist," as she had in "The Colossus"; and she opposes the "corpse" to a flowing stream nearby, whose waters recall "Lorelei" or "Full Fathom Five." All the qualities once assigned to the dead family and the colossal father are now attributed to the destroyed building: it is enormous in size; it is leathery and hard; it is stony; and it has been smashed into pieces. Plath's fondness for harsh alliterative sounds is put to brilliant use in "The Burnt-Out Spa":

The rafters and struts of his body wear
Their char of karakul still. I can't tell
How long his carcass has foundered under
The rubbish of summers, the blackleaved falls.

[*C*, p. 76]

We can almost see her delight in finding the word "karakul" (the curly black hair of the Karakul sheep) and placing it in conjunction with "char" and "carcass"; or her pleasure in drawing out this stanza, full of harsh *t*'s and *r*'s, with the long vowels and diphthongs of "blackleaved falls."

Plath opposes this corpse, which is composed of animal, human, statuary, and familial elements, to the living water that once flowed through the now-destroyed spa. The healing stream was evidently the reason for the existence of the spa, but it now only throws back her own unreal, static image to the poet. Leaning over the bridge that spans the stream, she says:

> I encounter one
> Blue and improbable person
>
> Framed in a basketwork of cattails.
> O she is gracious and austere,
> Seated beneath the toneless water!
> It is not I, it is not I.

[C, p. 77]

This narcissistic image below the water lives in a world of peace and harmony that the real self can never reach. In this last of the series of poems on the bodies of the dead, including "The Colossus," "Blue Moles," "Medallion," and "Mussel Hunter at Rock Harbor," Plath recognizes that she cannot escape into the waters of "Lorelei" and "Full Fathom Five." The world of the dead father and grandmother and of the past is shut: "And we shall never enter there," she says, "Where the durable ones keep house." The "durable ones" are the dead; their world is unavailable to her.

Plath's recognition that the world of stone and of the father was closed to her forever leads to the series of poems on self-transformation and rebirth, written in 1959, that culminate in "The Stones." These poems anticipate the initiatory movement that dominates the later work and foreshadow the stylistic changes that took place after Plath's move to England in the fall of 1959. The themes of birth and rebirth were linked in Plath's mind to three related issues that she had treated in poems written before 1959: changes in her perceptual state from one of "blankness" and "neutrality" to one of fluid and rich vision; alterations in normal physical shape or human form through magical or ritual process; and the shaping powers of art as it imposes design on raw material. The common denominator in these three issues is transformation. Perceptual, physical, and aesthetic changes all lead toward the creation of a new state of being.

Perceptual change occupied Plath as early as 1957 in "Black Rook in Rainy Weather," in which she had searched for a positive attitude toward the natural world. The self's "fear of total neutrality" can be overcome, the poem says, through vision. The visionary moment provides a complete transformation or metamorphosis of the world. The symbols for this heightened state are the black rook and the angel, whose "rare random descent" brings the poet hope in the midst of her fear. Similarly, "The Eye-Mote" (1958–59) locates the problem of living in the perceptual sphere: the speaker sees life as a rigid, unmoving entity. Based upon a real-life incident in which a splinter or speck lodged in Plath's eye, the poem connects the speaker's loss of perceptual clarity with her feelings of lost innocence, unhappiness, and sinfulness. The disturbance caused by the splinter and its medical removal has overtones of a fall from grace: "What I want back is what I was / Before the bed, before the knife . . . / Fixed me in this parenthesis" (*C*, p. 13). The title refers to the biblical parable of the mote and the beam (Luke 6:41), thus also linking the speaker's pained state to that of the sinner who suffers because he is blind to his own sin. She identifies herself with Oedipus, who blinded himself for his sins, and she prays for a return to her previous, more fluent state of being as opposed to her present state of fixity. Certainly "The Eye-Mote" raises more questions about the meaning of the speaker's references—to the mote itself, to the operation, to Oedipus—than it answers. But the opposition between stasis and movement, between rigid and fixed perception, will be the central focus in "Ariel."

Transformations resulting from aesthetic perception were discussed in "Medallion" and "Mussel Hunter at Rock Harbor." In those poems the dead are transfigured through aesthetic vision. But the most striking use of art as a means of transformation is "Sculptor" (1957–58), which is placed directly before the final poem sequence about rebirth, "Poem for a Birthday," in order to emphasize the theme of transformation. "Sculptor" takes up the same images of stone and hardness as the rest of *The Colossus*, but treats them in a completely different way. The poem describes the work of Leonard Baskin, who was artist-in-residence at Smith College while Plath was there. Art is seen as a transforming activity that can turn dead matter—bronze, wood, stone—into images of a world that transcends death. Baskin's sculptures, Plath says, provide "A solider repose than death's" (*C*, p. 79); and she expresses a certain contempt for those who have not given themselves over to Baskin's transforming process because they are "bodiless," that is, their bodies have no permanence of solidity. This view of art recalls the eternalizing theme in Renaissance sonnet sequences, but in Plath's hands it also places art within the context of the physical metamorphosis of the self. The new, solider shape that sculpture gives to the human body is akin to the reborn body that Plath imagines in the seven-part sequence.

Physical transformation and rebirth is, in fact, the direction and goal of *The Colossus*. Although only a few poems directly anticipate the physical changes of "Poem for a Birthday," almost all of *The Colossus*, as we have seen, deals with the body and its shape—from the corpses of "Two Views of a Cadaver Room" to the stone body of "The Colossus" to the broken building of "The Burnt-Out Spa." Plath's poetry is essentially a poetry of the body and of our imaginative perception of it. "Faun" (1956), for example, is one of the earliest poems in *The Colossus* to imagine a physical transformation. It depicts a metamorphosis along the Ovidian model: a mysterious change from human to animal takes place in the forest, observed only by the animals. Although the meaning of this change is not indicated by the poem, it anticipates Plath's later metamorphoses into the strange creatures of "Poem for a Birthday."

"Snakecharmer" (1957), which is based on a painting by

Henri Rousseau, also provides a framework for varied animal-human transformations. The snakecharmer is a kind of magician-artist, who creates a "snaky sphere": "He pipes. Pipes green. Pipes water." His control over a frightening aspect of nature attracts him to Plath, who is fascinated by the possibility of making and unmaking the physical shapes in which we find ourselves.

"Poem for a Birthday" is a compendium of physical changes. It subsumes all the elements that had appeared in the earlier poems on death—stones, moles, earthen wombs, water, mothers and fathers, frogs and animals. The central tendency of each of the individual poems, "Who," "Dark House," "Maenad," "The Beast," "Flute Notes from A Reedy Pond," "Witch Burning," and "The Stones," is regression to an earlier human or a nonhuman physical state. For example, in "Who" the speaker becomes a tiny, unnamed inhabitant of tool sheds and flower pots; in "Dark House," a molelike creature; in "Maenad," a confused and drunken follower of Dionysus; in "The Stones," a fetus inside the mother's womb. Plath thus reenvisions and resymbolizes in this poem the confrontation with death, the family, and nature that occupies all of the preceding poems. Instead of looking at the dead, though, either as animals, natural forms, corpses, family members, or women, Plath now *becomes* the objects she has feared: she turns into a mole ("Who"); becomes a stone ("The Stones"); dies as a witch on the stake ("Witch Burning"); goes underground into the landscape ("The Beast"). These physical transformations in the poetry convert what had once been merely a series of perceptual occasions into dramatic actions: the poet's persona now dramatizes a change in her being as if she had actually abandoned her normal physical condition.

The movement in *The Colossus* as a whole, then, is from objectification of the outside world to identification with central parts of it. "Poem for a Birthday" celebrates a birthday by imagining a series of deathlike transformations, which it then converts into rebirths. To take one example, "Flute Notes from a Reedy Pond" is spoken by a creature who lives near a pond. The covering reeds of summer are withering "like pithless hands" (*C*, p. 84). Much of nature is about to go to sleep for the winter, and the speaker's plaintive tone suggests Plath's sense of resignation in the face of natural cycles. But the death process, which seems to occur among the worms, the reeds, and the insects, is not really death: "This is not death, it is something safer." By identifying with a nonhuman form of life, Plath in effect affirms a cycle of death and rebirth that moves from winter to spring and back again. According to the poem, this rebirth of spring is akin to Christ's; the waters of the pond are the "waters of golgotha."

The final poem, "The Stones," is the fitting end to the thematic drama of *The Colossus*. Throughout the volume the resistant, ungiving force in the world is stone: the stone Colossus, the grandmother's egg-stones, the Hardcastle Crags, the stony muses, and Egg Rock. The natural and the human, including family members, had been turned to stone; but in the final poem of the volume the poet herself becomes stone, as if to show that death had trapped the poet's self as well. "The Stones" turns the drama of petrification, which Plath had presented as the fate of those outside her, into the self's own struggle.

"The Stones" also recapitulates the motifs in the other sections of "Poem for a Birthday": regression to an immobile, fetuslike state; the baneful influence of the mother; and the concern with eating. All these elements are overcome in the transformation that turns the poet into a baby: "My swaddled legs and arms smell sweet as rubber" (*C*, p. 83). By gaining a new body, Plath symbolically turns her back upon the world of stone and of death. Love, she says, has been her "curse"; she looks forward to the moment when her love will be directed more toward the living than toward the dead. In her "reconstructed vase," which represents her new body, she places the "elusive rose," the sense of beauty and wholeness that she periodically loses. The theme of rebirth, with its ambiguous relation to the desire for death, has tended toward the final line of "The Stones": "I shall be good as new"—an unfortunately weak ending to an otherwise good poem.

Perhaps the process of regeneration would be more convincing if the poem had not ended on that weak line; but Plath had not yet come to the intense conviction, manifested throughout the later work, that her survival depended upon self-transformation. Several critics have read the final line of "The Stones" as an ironic commentary on the futility of returning to a "normal" life that appears hollow and boring to the poet. But "irony" is hardly the right word to apply here, since it suggests a control over the alternatives of death and life that Plath nowhere possesses. It would be ironic if Plath could, at this point, reject her desire to be "good as new" and accept the futility of her quest for rebirth, but she can no more do this than she can achieve, in any permanent form, the sought-after change in physical shape. We must thus read the final line of *The Colossus* as the simultaneous testimony to two contradictory emotional desires: to be reborn into a totally "new" self and to retain the "old" self with its hatred for itself and all others.

Thematic order in *The Colossus* consists, then, in the balancing of contradictory realities: the objectified, often hostile environment of wild animals, stone, landscape and seascape, dead family members, and corpses, with the desired life of the lost childhood, the mythical underwater kingdom, and the transforming power of art. Plath's repetition of the same images in poem after poem—stone, sea, sun and moon, animals—suggests the constancy of the themes of death and rebirth in her work. She chooses the same kinds of landscapes and the same individuals (the father, the spinster, the mother) again and again. If one poem seems best to exemplify the thematic tension of the volume as a whole, it is the title poem in which the despairing and resigned daughter confronts a landscape of hard, fragmented marble and admits that she cannot make Greek stone come alive and assume the shape of her father. But the imagery of "The Colossus" contradicts in part its final abandonment of all hope, since the daughter does not completely forget the Colossus: she still sleeps in his left ear, taking refuge in a fragmented memory of the past.

four

Landscapes and Bodyscapes

The poems of *The Colossus* were obviously selected and arranged to highlight thematic groupings and to set off thematic polarities. But Plath was unable to fix upon an overall organization for the poetry written from 1960 through 1963. Ted Hughes reports that the poems of 1960–61 had several different manuscript titles and that Plath could never settle on a selection of poems.[1] Although she had begun to choose poems for the *Ariel* volume before she died, she did not live to assemble that book either.[2] As a consequence, the volumes represent neither the ordering intention of the poet nor the sequential pattern of chronology. The four books of later poetry, *Crossing the Water*, *Pursuit*, *Ariel*, and *Winter Trees*, each contain poems from different periods of Plath's career; only *Ariel* seems to approach the shape of a finished book. It thus seems necessary, before a discussion of the later poetry, to place Plath's work in its temporal sequence.

Ted Hughes is correct to suggest that a crucial stylistic development occurred in the later work at the beginning of 1962 with the composition of "Elm" and "The Moon and the Yew Tree."[3] Dividing her later work, then, into transitional poetry (1960–61) and late poetry (1962–63) provides an easily manageable framework in which to place her widely dispersed poems. Of the transitional poems, twenty-eight are printed in *Crossing the Water*. Almost all of them were published in 1960 through 1962 in British magazines, *London Magazine*, *New Statesman*, *The Observer*, *Critical Quarterly*, and *The Listener*, or American magazines, *The New Yorker* and *Poetry*.[4]

Pursuit contains "The Rival (2)," which was written in July 1961, as well as some early work and five late poems: "Words Heard, by Accident, Over the Phone," "Stings (2)," "The Fearful," "A Secret," and "Burning the Letters." Five poems included in *Ariel* date from the transitional period: "Tulips," "Morning Song," "You're," and "Little Fugue." "You're" was written just before the birth of Plath's first child in April 1960. "Tulips" is a companion poem to "In Plaster," which is in *Crossing the Water*; both were composed in March 1961 at the time of Plath's appendectomy. According to Ted Hughes, "Morning Song" and "Little Fugue" date from late 1961.

Of the approximately sixty-two late poems, thirty-eight are in *Ariel*, seventeen are in *Winter Trees*, plus the radio play *Three Women*, and five are in *Pursuit*.[5] "The Jailor" has not yet been published in book form.[6] Of the *Ariel* poems, "Elm," "The Moon and the Yew Tree" and "Berck Plage" were written between April and July 1962. The bee sequence came in October, as did some of the poems set off by Plath's thirtieth birthday on 27 October: "Lady Lazarus" and "A Birthday Present." Poems of mid-January included "The Hanging Man," "Years," "The Munich Mannequins," "Totem," "Paralytic," and "Poppies in July." The final week of Plath's life produced the five poems at the end of *Ariel*: "Balloons," "Contusion," "Kindness," "Edge," and "Words." *Three Women* was written in the spring of 1962 and performed in August of that year; and the poems in *Pursuit* range from August to October 1962.

It is clear from this chronology that Plath completed the late poems with incredible rapidity. Most of them were finished within four months' time: October through January and a small part of February. As a result, there is a high degree of consistency in thematic and imagistic elements in the late poems, particularly in the representation of nature and in the use of natural images. In moving toward a poetry of initiation, Plath rapidly altered both her use of nature images and her perception of the external world. The transitional poems are largely landscapes and seascapes in which Plath experiments with variable line lengths and open forms in an effort to penetrate the world outside her and to create a more personal form of poetry.

The most significant development in Plath's poetry from *The Colossus* to the transitional and late poems relates directly to her internalization of images and objects that she had previously treated impersonally. Her handling of landscapes and sea-scapes indicates that she intensified her identification with external objects and scenes in order to use them as immediate symbols or correlatives of mental states. In *The Colossus*, Plath's relationship to the natural world was split between the modes of objectification and identification. "Blue Moles," for example, shows how the dead can be both hard objects and sympathetic beings. In the transitional work, Plath is halfway to a complete identification with what she sees. Landscapes are perceived in terms of the human body or of human artifacts. The external world becomes an accurate imagistic equivalent for states of mind. Eventually, in the late work, the landscapes and sea-scapes merge so completely with the perceiving self that they are converted into extensions of the body, and every external description refers back to the relation between the poet and her own physical existence.

"Blackberrying" is representative of these transitional land-scapes, and it can be used to show the mood and method of the transitional works as a whole. The emotional focus of the poem is nature's roughness and unyieldingness, a theme al-ready considered in a poem like "Hardcastle Crags" in *The Colossus*. The difference between the earlier and later treatments, however, is significant. "Blackberrying" is a first-person, not a third-person, narrative that develops images of the body and of nature in a much more forceful and frightening way than did "Hardcastle Crags." The blackberries become symbols of blood, and the thorns of the berry bushes are repeatedly spoken of as "hooks." The juxtaposition of references to blood and hooks with body references ("thumb," "eyes," "fingers," "face") turns this landscape into a meditation on natural and bodily destructiveness.

The three nine-line stanzas of "Blackberrying" demonstrate

an ordered, three-step progression in the speaker's walk to the sea down a path lined with blackberry bushes. As she collects the berries in a milk bottle, she compares them to parts of the body; they are "Big as the ball of my thumb, and dumb as eyes" (CW, p. 13). Their red juice is, figuratively, human blood, and the speaker imagines herself joined in a "Blood sisterhood" with the berries. This imaginative kinship with blood berries is hardly unique in Plath's poetry. In "Ariel" the horsewoman speaks of berries casting "dark / Hooks— / Black sweet blood mouthfuls" (A, p. 26). "Years" contains the line: "The blood berries are themselves, they are very still" (A, p. 72). In each of these cases the poet seems to identify with the vulnerable, animate form in the midst of a hostile nature. The berries thus become internalized objects; they symbolize the fate of human beings who are "eaten" by the universe, a metaphor Plath employs time and again in the late poetry. The speaker wishes to establish a very special relation with the berries and with the landscape; it is as if the natural scene had been transformed into a human body and she were commenting on that body's condition.

The second stanza shifts the focus of the poem from the berries to other natural elements—birds, sea, meadow, flies— all of which possess a certain deadness. The birds, for example, appear as "Bits of burnt white paper wheeling in a blown sky." This conversion of the natural into the artificial is, of course, characteristic of Plath's handling of nature in The Colossus.

The "burnt white paper" suggests both destruction and blankness. When the narrator of the poem speaks of the flies on the berry bush as hanging "their wing panes in a Chinese screen," she is again suggesting the artificiality of the world in which she lives. The flies, in fact, act not so much like flies as like gorged men after a meal. The whole stanza, with its end-stopped, low-keyed lines, indicates a disjointedness and lack of vitality in nature.

The final stanzas present the sea as a powerful and gigantic nothingness with awesome, though meaningless, power. The speaker is brought to this vision as if deliberately by the environment: the wind "slaps" her face; a "hook" from a berry bush brings her forward to the ocean as if intentionally. She then perceives the alternative to the land:

A last hook brings me
To the hills' northern face, and the face is orange rock
That looks out on nothing, nothing but a great space
Of white and pewter lights, and a din like silversmiths
Beating and beating at an intractable metal.

[*CW*, p. 13]

The sea is obviously a disappointment: it is "nothing," a play of light and sound. Although the metaphor of silversmithing as applied to the waves beating on the shore might have been a vehicle for Romantic doctrine on creative nature, in Plath's hands it becomes an expression of nature's randomness and meaninglessness. Where she expects a transforming spirit, she finds only an absence. The sea becomes an "intractable metal" that will not take on a humanly meaningful shape. Unlike the blackberries, which Plath converted into "sisters," the sea resists all comforting anthropomorphic interpretation.

Two significant differences separate "Blackberrying" from the poems of *The Colossus*. First, the metaphors of the poem are linked more through associative than logical processes. In the earlier poems, Plath tended to fix on a single metaphor, as in "The Colossus" or "Hardcastle Crags," and develop it through a progression of logical stages. But in the transitional landscapes she begins to free herself from the concept of the single metaphor or conceit as the framework for the poem. She now sees metaphors as temporary indicators of a mental state: they must inevitably give way to new stages in the mental process. The landscape thus appears as a mental construction of the poet rather than as an objectively perceived external scene. The metaphors and similes of "Blackberrying" correspond more closely to the momentary perceptions of the speaker than do the metaphors of *The Colossus* poems: blackberries as hooks, birds as bits of paper, the waves as silversmiths.

Second, the mood in "Blackberrying" is less confident and buoyant than in *The Colossus*. The abandonment of traditional stanza forms and rhyme schemes as well as Plath's willingness to associate images more freely appears to have allowed her to open up disturbing personal material. *The Colossus* includes mainly poems of natural menace and danger, yet it gives the impression—principally because of its formal regularity and literary diction—of the poet's control over the hostile external forces. This control becomes increasingly less apparent in the poems after 1959. Plath permits herself the expression of irrational elements that cannot be confined within symmetrical structures. In *Ariel* and *Winter Trees*, the sense of being overwhelmed and victimized by an irrational world has taken over, and the poem no longer presents a structure that creates distance from the disorder of the universe. Form comes to reflect the speaker's violent war with the world and with others.

Although the transitional landscapes are more open to the personal situation of the poet than are the earlier landscapes and seascapes, they fail to make the natural scene they describe meaningful in relation to a specific personality. Thus it is often difficult to know how to respond to certain natural images or what particular issue the images focus on. Still, these transitional poems have extraordinary individual lines and images and, almost always, a coherent tone. They are much more subtle than the corresponding *Colossus* poems in their imagistic and emotional effects, yet they often leave the reader waiting for an intellectual or emotional resolution.

In "Wuthering Heights," for example, the landscape is the forbidding moors of Emily Bronte's novel that Plath had previously used in "Hardcastle Crags"; but the poem never becomes more than a study in mood. The speaker feels vulnerable, and she identifies with fragile aspects of natural life, with grass blown by the wind, and with sheep. Plath stresses nature's indifference: "Of people the air only / Remembers a few odd syllables" (*CW*, p. 2). At the close of the poem, however, there is not so much a resolution as a fade-out. Darkness falls on the grass, terrifying it; in the distance the house lights of the town gleam. As in "Blackberrying," the play of dark and light fascinates the speaker, but it is unclear what meaning to attach to it. The vulnerability and passivity of the speaker are all that seem indicated by the numerous interesting and well-handled natural images.

The persistence of the mood of "Blackberrying" and "Wuthering Heights" deserves note. The same elements that have already been mentioned reappear in "Finisterre," which describes the rocky shoreline off the coast of France. The rocks are treated in terms of body images: they are "rheumatic" fingers and "leftover soldiers from old, messy wars" (*CW*, p. 3). Nature is once again harsh and indifferent to the human world, and religion is of no help. A giant marble statue of Our Lady of the Shipwrecked is an object of devotion. As with the unresponsive Colossus, however, the statue does not show the slightest interest in the plight of the people: "She [the statue] does not hear what the sailor or peasant is saying— / She is in love with the beautiful formlessness of the sea." The sea stands for nature's colossal unruliness, as it does in "Blackberrying."

The perception of nature as a void or nothingness, which appeared in the last image of "Blackberrying," is the dominant notion of "Private Ground." This description of the Yaddoo estate in New York State, where Plath and her husband stayed in the fall of 1959, focuses on a drained fish basin in which the dead fish lie. When the speaker collects the fish and throws them into a nearby lake, she seems to be offering to the water the debris of human reality as well as animal life: "Morgue of old logs and old images, the lake / Opens and shuts, accepting them among its reflections" (*CW*, p. 21). Like the sea, the lake is a totally indifferent world, accepting uncaringly both images (human productions) and logs. Other images in the poem recall elements previously mentioned: the grass is again a symbol of the grieving, delicate natural object; the dead baby carp suffer a metaphoric transformation into orange peels that remind one of the gorged flies of "Blackberrying."

The indifference of nature becomes pure hostility in "Sleep in the Mojave Desert," a landscape based on Plath's trip to the Southwest in 1959. The dominant mood here is determined by images of heat ("The sun puts its heat out") and by the projection of human feeling onto the insects: "The heat-cracked crickets congregate / In their black armorplate and cry" (*CW*, p. 29). This landscape remains undeveloped, however; we never learn what the speaker particularly feels in relation to it. In contrast, "Two Campers in Cloud Country," which is set in Rock Lake, Canada, does account for the transformation of the speaker's inner life as she confronts nature. Without the comforts of history or civilization, she feels herself turning into a numb, selfless body. As in "Finisterre," rocks are symbols of nature's indifference; and as in much of *The Colossus*, the loss of identity is noted by use of the adjective "blank": "We'll wake blank-brained in the dawn" (*CW*, p. 33). The feeling of this poem is certainly different from the mood of *The Colossus*; the blankness of the speaker is no longer a negative experience. She says that it is even "comfortable, for a change, to mean so little." The image of blankness now refers to the purity of consciousness that results from the initiatory descent into the darkness of the material world. Plath is describing one aspect of the ritual process of disintegration and renewal.

Another poem written about Plath's Canadian experience, "Crossing the Water," emphasizes "the spirit of blackness" in nature and man. The poem anticipates the later landscapes in its repetition of color images and its laconic style. Almost every line of its triadic stanzas is end-stopped, suggesting the lack of continuity in the speaker's perception of the water scene. Moving across the blackness of a lake, the speaker and her companion lose their substantiality and merge into the silence of the natural scene. A mood of darkness and expectancy is conjured up by the poem and then suddenly dropped, as if the whole point of the poem were to convey a moment of astonishment at natural beauty before it vanished in the darkness.

A truly negative response to a land- and seascape dominates "Whitsun," a description of a holiday trip to the beach in England. Plath compares the natural world to people or objects that she dislikes. The sea, for example, has the "glaucous silks" of an obsequious Oriental; a cliff becomes a green pool table; rocks are petrified eggs. Degenerate and deadening, the seascape is simply *there*, leaving the speaker and her companion seasick on the beach.

The final transitional landscapes, "Parliament Hill Fields" and "Stars over the Dordogne," are meditative excursions into different aspects of nature. "Parliament Hill Fields" is set in the Hampstead Heath area of London, where Plath lived in 1961. The speaker is a mother who apparently has lost a child through miscarriage.[7] Although many of the references in this poem remain obscure, it is clear that the speaker finds solace in the pale, fog-bound landscape because it so closely mirrors her feelings of loss and isolation. The natural world is treated through images of man-made objects: the sky is "Faceless and pale as china"; the birds, as in "Blackberrying," are pieces of paper; and the wind is "like a bandage" (*CW*, p. 7). The poem refers to a family situation that the speaker has momentarily left behind her—a daughter's room, marriage difficulties—without specifying in any detail what her situation is. Like the other landscape poems of this time, "Parliament Hill Fields" only partially develops the personal significance of the natural scene, never fully using nature as a precise symbolic language that could reveal the self.

"Stars over the Dordogne" approximates to a degree the technique used in the later landscape poems. It compares the night sky over southern France with the speaker's memory of starry nights in New England. As in "The Moon and the Yew Tree," this kind of poem tends to internalize the external world. The stars over France are more numerous and more exciting than those over America; but the persona turns inward to the "puritan and solitary" American stars: "And where I lie now, back to my own dark star, / I see those constellations [from the New England sky] in my head, / Unwarmed by the sweet air of this peach orchard."[8] The contrast between the moods of French and American nights leads only to a stated preference for the sparse night sky of America; yet the poem has a wistful mood and graceful flow, indicating Plath's mastery of the nine-line stanza and variable five-, six- or seven-beat line.

The transitional landscapes are characterized, then, by Plath's use of natural metaphors for mental states. But she has not yet found in these poems a method for applying these metaphors to personality and to the initiatory scenario through which the self must pass. She discovers a "plot" that will allow her to dramatize the interrelations between self and nature and self and others in the writing of such landscapes as "The Moon and the Yew Tree" and "Apprehensions," where she totally internalizes the external objects of the earlier poems. In most of the later landscapes and seascapes, natural images are a shorthand for aspects of personality. Ted Hughes has correctly emphasized the importance of "The Moon and the Yew Tree" in Plath's development of this method. The poem is particularly important because it combines two types of poems that had been important in *The Colossus*: poems about father and mother ("The Colossus," "The Disquieting Muses") and poems about nature. The fusion of these concerns can take place because Plath now perceives all objects—whether human, animate, or inanimate—in terms of a system of metaphorical-symbolic equations. The system is not rigid, but its general elements are consistently used by Plath. "The Moon and the Yew Tree" can serve as a primary example of her incorporation of natural objects in a symbolic system.

The occasion for the writing of "The Moon and the Yew Tree," according to Ted Hughes, was a scene outside of the Hughes's house in Devon, England. The cemetery across from the house, the yew tree in front of the cemetery, and the full moon overhead triggered the poem; but its actual subject is the sense of doom that overhangs Plath's inner landscape. As the first line tells us, the light of the moon is "the light of the mind, cold and planetary" (*A*, p. 41). Within this mental light, the natural objects represent images of mother and father. The moon is identified as the poet's mother, full of despair; the black yew tree, from what we know of its other uses, with the poet's father. The tree points to the moon, but the moon does not open up to any possibility other than the bleak scene before the poet. "The moon," says Plath, "is no door." Each of the colors in the landscape (black, white, blue) takes on a specific personal meaning as the poem progresses. Black is the father's color, indicating the silence of the dead; white is the mother's color, indicating despair and the fear of death; and blue is the Virgin Mary's color, indicating hopefulness.

In contrast to the personal signs of despair (moon, yew tree) in stanzas 1 and 2 are the symbols of the religious tradition in stanzas 2 and 4 that promise afterlife and salvation. The poem mentions the bells that ring out on Sunday, "affirming the Resurrection." In the third stanza, Plath contrasts the white moon-mother, who is "bald and wild," with the blue mother of Christ, Mary, who is tender. The face of Mary, "gentled by candles," then replaces the moon's face, which was "White as a knuckle and terribly upset." A new series of colors and images has thus supplanted the original sequence. A religious fantasia appears in the place of the bleak world:

> Inside the church, the saints will be all blue,
> Floating on their delicate feet over the cold pews,
> Their hands and faces still with holiness.
> The moon sees nothing of this. She is bald and wild.
> And the message of the yew tree is blackness—
> blackness and silence.

Plath has codified the natural world; colors and images are "messages" sent by the world to the poet, speaking of the poet's personal condition. The natural scene of the cemetery, pointing yew tree and blank moon, is not so much an external scene as a combination of ancient images that designate the poet's inner world. By then symbolizing an alternate, positive sequence of images—Mary, blueness, saints—Plath creates a dynamic conflict between two mental realities. The ordinary sense of boundaries between nonhuman and human, between external and internal, fails to hold here; Plath's mother *is* the moon, and the blue saints occupy their own actual church. Plath has moved fluidly from a despairing natural landscape to a hopeful "inscape," as Gerard Manley Hopkins called it. None of the *Colossus* poems shows this movement, nor possesses the grace and sureness with which to execute it.

The central colors of "The Moon and the Yew Tree" (black, white, blue) and elements (trees, moon, Mary) reappear throughout the late poems. The technique of treating objects and colors as coded messages to the self gives the best of the landscapes their distinctiveness. As was shown in the discussion of "The Rabbit Catcher" and "Getting There" in chapter 2, the landscape of death in Plath's later poems provides the initial framework for the dramatic action of initiation. In "The Moon and the Yew Tree," Plath makes a key step toward the ritual participation of the self in the death-and-life process of the universe. The self is trapped in a world that "speaks" to it incessantly of personal issues through natural objects: the moon's appearance in the sky is the presence of a controlling, dominating mother; the blackness of the trees is the absence of a loved, though feared, father; and the Virgin Mary is a "good mother," who provides the element of salvation from the hopeless confrontation between male and female principles. As in "Fever 103°," the Virgin provides an image of transformation that stands as a spiritual alternative to the world of death. "The Moon and the Yew Tree" does not offer a dynamic movement to rebirth, but it marks the moment in a career (April 1962) when Plath combines the language of her landscape poetry with the obsessive images and concerns of her poems about the family.

By establishing a hermetic language of images, Plath was able to write a personal poetry that retains an objective character. This procedure is evident in "Apprehensions," which deals with fears of childbirth without ever directly mentioning its personal subject. The poem is structured through associations to four colored walls in a hospital room: white, gray, red, and black. On one level of significance, the colors reflect the changing light patterns during the course of a day, from early morning (white) through afternoon cloudiness (gray), sunset (red), and nightfall (black). On a second, more internalized level, they indicate perceptual environments. The white wall is a screen for images of the unattainable external world: sky, stars, angels, and dissolving sunlight. The bloody gray wall is a projection screen for images of the mind; the red wall, for images of the body, and the black wall, for images of death. In each case, the walls are like the landscapes of "The Moon and the Yew Tree": they "speak" to the poet about the condition in which she finds herself.

The "Apprehensions" referred to in the title are apprehensions of death in childbirth. The third stanza, which concentrates on "the red fist, opening and closing," suggests the contractions of the uterus (*WT*, p. 3). The "Two grey, papery bags" are the ovaries. And the speaker's "terror / Of being wheeled off under crosses and a rain of pieties" indicates that she is in a hospital, afraid of being taken off to die. Like "Tulips," this poem deals with the terrors awakened by physical discomfort in a hospital through sequences of images associated with different colors. The wall of the hospital room serves as a screen onto which to project her fear that there is no escape from death and from the mind's imagination of death. "Apprehensions" expresses exactly the same sense of entrapment and despair that "The Moon and the Yew Tree" does; in the latter poem, Plath says: "I simply cannot see where there is

to get to," meaning that death closes all avenues of escape.
Here she asks, in the second stanza, "Is there no way out of the
mind?" and answers, in the final stanza, that there is not:

> On a black wall, unidentifiable birds
> Swivel their heads and cry.
> There is no talk of immortality among these!
> Cold blanks approach us:
> They move in a hurry.
>
> [*WT*, p. 3]

When death approaches, it is a blankness, an absence at the
heart of reality that sweeps across the world and obliterates all
color, warmth, and life. It is also significant that the pronoun
of this final stanza is no longer first-person singular but first-
person plural, thus indicating the universality of the death
world.

A similar mood and technique as in "The Moon and the Yew
Tree" and "Apprehensions" governs "Sheep in Fog." This
short, sensitive lyric contrasts an external landscape with the
imagined, and feared, landscape of heaven. Unlike "The Moon
and the Yew Tree," the religious imagery does not give com-
fort; rather, it embodies the fear that the afterlife is a dark
nothingness. As the poet looks out over white sheep covering a
hillside early one morning, she feels disappointed in herself.
The white world of the sheep and the white clouds of smoke
given off by a nearby train induce in her a mood of sadness: the
deepening fog seems to portend the obliteration of the scene in
front of her. Suddenly, she switches from the white landscape
of the morning to an inner landscape:

> My bones hold a stillness, the far
> Fields melt my heart.
>
> They threaten
> To let me through to a heaven
> Starless and fatherless, a dark water.
>
> [*A*, p. 3]

Underlying the world of sheep and trains, the poet fears, is not Father in his starry heaven but a dark, undifferentiated ocean of nothingness. The absent father is both the poet's dead father and the dead God of religion; and from their environment of blackness and starlessness, the poet can expect nothing at all. Landscape, blackness, and self are thus merged in a final image of nothingness that recalls the ending of "The Moon and the Yew Tree." The initial stage of initiation—the entry into the death world—has thus been accomplished.

Another equation of landscape with mental state is "Lyonnesse." According to Arthurian legend, the area called Lyonnesse, between Cornwall and the Scilly Islands, suddenly sank into the sea one day. Plath's poem is thus, paradoxically, about an absent landscape; the land area as well as the people who lived on it have been destroyed. In the poem, Plath attributes this conversion of a landscape into a seascape to the work of God. The ocean, she imagines, is God's mind; and the Lyonians have actually discovered heaven: "The Lyonians had always thought that / Heaven would be something else" (*WT*, p. 30). As in "Sheep in Fog," heaven is blackness and absence: "The white gape of his [God's] mind was the real Tabula Rasa." The familiar natural environment is replaced by the blank slate of God or—what is the same in Plath's vision—death.

An extension of the landscape technique to the body is apparent in "Contusion" and "Edge," two poems of Plath's last week. The landscape becomes a "bodyscape"; the poet treats the body as if it were external to her self. In "Contusion," she compares the inner life of the wounded body to three physical processes: the movement of the sea over rock, the motion of a fly on a wall, and the covering of mirrors with sheets after death. Bodily processes are thus compared to external phenomena. It is as if the human body were literally the sea and death were the sliding back of the water from its normal position. The poem makes no distinction between the external and the internal; metaphorically, the seascape and the bodyscape are one. Similarly, in "Edge," the body of a dead woman, with her two dead children, is described as a flower in a pastoral garden scene:

> She has folded
> Them [the children] back into her body as petals
> Of a rose close when the garden
>
> Stiffens and odours bleed
> From the sweet, deep throats of the night flower.
>
> [*A*, p. 84]

The woman metaphorically becomes the rose; her children, the petals; and both woman and children are absorbed in the sweetness of the garden. Needless to say, the entire process of identification in "Edge" forms part of a suicidal drive. As in "The Moon and the Yew Tree," the moon hovers over the landscape of death and despair, indifferent to and distant from the drama below. The moon indicates that there is nowhere "to get to." The descent into darkness in the landscapes is one with the drive to abolish the conflicting reality of the self.

Three other landscapes make use of the flower as a central symbol for the poet's inner situation; each stresses the identity of nature and human body. "Poppies in October" and "Poppies in July" are companion pieces describing two antithetical stages in Plath's reaction to the complex image of the poppy. "Poppies in October" emphasizes the magnificence of the red flower: its aliveness amid the frozen natural world (the "forest of frost") and amid the death-haunted human world (the woman being taken off in an ambulance to the hospital). According to the color symbolism, redness represents blood, the life force. In a personal world filled with death-fears, the poet gives thanks that she can witness the brilliance of the poppies: "O my God, what am I / That these late mouths should cry open / In a forest of frost, in a dawn of cornflowers" (*A*, p. 19). By speaking of the flowers as "mouths," Plath has both humanized the poppies and given them the power to "speak" for her love of natural brilliance and power.

Similarly, in "Poppies in July," the poppies are red mouths; but now the intensity of the flowers' life seems too great for the speaker to bear. She is exhausted by the sight of the poppies "Flickering like that, wrinkly and clear red, like the skin of a mouth" (*A*, p. 81). She therefore wants to forget her own existence either by becoming the flower or by swallowing the opium derivative of the poppies. A different level of symbolism related to the flowers emerges: "If I could bleed, or sleep— / If my mouth could marry a hurt like that! / Or your liquors seep to me, in this glass capsule." Through identification with the flower or through the act of swallowing its essence, the poet hopes to escape from the crisis of her life, to merge with the natural world.

A less interesting poem than the previous two, "Among the Narcissi" continues the metaphorical identification of human beings with flowers. The situation of the octogenarian Percy is equated with that of the narcissus flowers. Percy has apparently been in the hospital; and what he has suffered, the flowers also suffer: "The flowers vivid as bandages, and the man mending. / They bow and stand: they suffer such attacks!" (*WT*, p. 15). The "attacks" from the wind and from the external world unite the vulnerable man with the vulnerable flower. Unfortunately, Plath does not develop the connection in any substantial way in this poem.

The landscape of "Winter Trees" is outwardly more promising than the seascape of "Lyonnesse," but its fertility only reminds the speaker of what she, as a woman, lacks. Absence is again made the dominant theme of the landscape. The three stanzas develop three related aspects of fertility: the symbolic "wedding" of the past and future of trees through the formation of rings; the effortless germination of seeds; and the motherly and divine quality of the Ledalike trees. In comparison with the organic rootedness and innocence of the trees, women seem devoted to sterility ("abortions") and cruelty ("bitchery"). The poem contrasts the pure, organic spontaneity of the natural world with the tortured, inauthentic life of women. The poet can perceive the wonder of the trees, but she cannot participate in it. At the end of the poem she sees and hears the "shadows of ringdoves chanting," but the perception cannot ease her pain. She is shut out from the natural universe.

The connection between the theme of woman's fertility and the symbolism of trees appears also in "Childless Woman," where the infertile woman projects her own landscape in order to reflect the barrenness of her body. Both woman and tree attempt to fertilize the world, the woman unsuccessfully:

> The womb
> Rattles its pod, the moon
> Discharges itself from the tree with nowhere to go.
>
> My landscape is a hand with no lines,
> The roads bunched to a knot,
> The knot myself, . . .
>
> [*WT*, p. 34]

The "knotted" palm of the childless woman is her body's landscape. She then converts her own body into a landscape of death, in which she herself is the burial ground for the "mirrors" of her self, that is, the ova, which she vainly produces.

"Letter in November" is the least internalized of all the landscapes that have been considered. It is also one of the most difficult to describe because of its allusiveness. Plath seems to be unifying two opposed worlds, history and nature. As she walks about her garden, she feels comforted, as in "Poppies in October," by the beauty of the organic world:

> The streetlight
> Splits through the rat's-tail
> Pods of the laburnum at nine in the morning.
> It is the Arctic,
>
> This little black
> Circle, with its tawn silk grasses—babies' hair.

There is a green in the air,
Soft, delectable.
It cushions me lovingly.

[*A*, p. 46]

The warmth of the natural scene is so great that she even feels at home with the dead who lie buried nearby and with the fog that symbolizes those who have died throughout history, the "thick grey death-soup." Yet the contrast between the immediate beauty of the gold apples and the terrifying vision of history leads not to despair but to elation; she feels isolated and triumphant as she walks through her garden. The mysterious last line of the poem converts the gold apples into the bodies of those who died in one of the great battles of antiquity: "The irreplaceable / Golds bleed and deepen, the mouths of Thermopylae." In "Letter in November," then, landscape unifies the dead and the natural in one vision, and the speaker attains a state of happiness by loving the scene before her.

As in *The Colossus*, the attitudes toward nature in the transitional and late poems derive from conflicting, often absolutely antithetical, perceptions of the sea and the land. The degenerate seascape of "Whitsun," the desolate land- and seascape of "Finisterre," the codified natural world of "The Moon and the Yew Tree," seem to be incompatible with the wonderful night sky of "Stars over the Dordogne," the brilliance of the red "Poppies in October," or the comforting tree landscape of "Letter in November." Plath was not interested in a consistent view of the natural, but in a true one; and the truth that her best landscapes and seascapes reveal is the inextricable mixture of death and life, the negative and the positive, within human existence. The internalization of the natural world; the adoption of private symbolic meanings for red, white, and black, for tree, moon, and sea; the conversion of a positive symbol into an image of death, or vice versa—all these represent Plath's desire to fuse the external and internal worlds into a "language" for the self. In "The Moon and the Yew Tree,"

"Apprehensions," "Edge," and "Sheep in Fog," this fusion is most successful, and we seem to experience simultaneously the beautiful sensate world and its power for destruction and death. Though they are not her best poems, the landscapes and bodyscapes represent the point at which Plath's vision of nature and her vision of self fuse into a personal language. The ultimate expression of this language lies in the poems that take her into the world of death and beyond it.

five

The World of Death

Plath's late poems dramatize the transformation of her personal situation into a metaphor for universal struggle. Although her critics continue to comb the poems for specific biographical references, the importance of Plath's work lies precisely in her alteration and heightening of autobiographical experience. In fact, we can distinguish between her successes and failures on the basis of her objectification of personal experiences through image sequences and metaphoric development. Thus, poems like "Words Heard, by Accident, Over the Phone" and "Burning the Letters" offer nothing more than a commentary on incidents from Plath's life; their metaphors must be read exclusively in terms of what happened to the poet on a certain day when she discovered her husband's infidelity or burned his letters because of his infidelity. The metaphors of these poems lack any larger relevance or reference. On the whole, though, her last poems successfully objectify the poet's relationship to four aspects of reality: to the family, to women, to nature, and to death. Ultimately, these relationships all center upon conflicting visions of death. We have already seen how the landscapes and seascapes provide Plath with the symbolic settings for the initiatory drama of life and death. Similarly, the poems about the family represent the split nature of her universe; they talk about destructive parents and the Holy Family, about death-haunted generations and innocent children. Women as well are perceived in antithetical ways; they appear at once as oppressors and as spiritual beings, as vicious enemies and as pure victims. The world of death, with its central symbols of the sea, the black sky, and the God-Father, provides the framework for the violent antagonism of these opposites. In Plath's universe, life always stands opposed to darkness and loss.

The fluid imagistic method of the last poems provides Plath's central means for objectifying her personal vision. A good example is "The Couriers," a brief, brilliant lyric that can also serve as an introduction to Plath's approach to marriage and the family.

> The word of a snail on the plate of a leaf?
> It is not mine. Do not accept it.
>
> Acetic acid in a sealed tin?
> Do not accept it. It is not genuine.
>
> A ring of gold with the sun in it?
> Lies. Lies and a grief.
>
>
> Frost on a leaf, the immaculate
> Cauldron talking and crackling
>
> All to itself on the top of each
> Of nine black Alps:
>
> A disturbance in mirrors,
> The sea shattering its grey one—
>
>
> Love, love, my season.
>
> [*A*, p. 2]

Although one critic has called it a "baffling poem," "The Couriers" can be explained fairly simply.[1] The poem has the double object of dissociating the poet from the symbols of married life and of projecting a vision of love outside of marriage. Two groups of three stanzas are followed by a final one-line stanza. The first group rejects symbols of domesticity, the snail on a leaf, the tin of acetic acid or vinegar, and the gold ring; the second group affirms the poet's countersymbols, frost on a leaf, the burning cauldron on mountain tops, and the violent surface of the sea; and the final stanza stresses the poet's triumphant ability to love in her own fashion. Thus "The Couriers" deals with the polarity of static domesticity and the charged dynamic world of the self that concerns several *Ariel* poems.

The mysterious couriers of the poem's title bring the opposing symbolic messages to the reader, who is instructed by the poet not to accept the first set of images. The first three images condense the values and qualities of married life that the speaker has come to detest. The snail on a leaf stands for the sluggish and dull domestic life; the sealed tin of vinegar symbolizes the enclosure and "sourness" of marriage; and the gold ring represents the wedding ring with its lying promise of bliss ("the sun in it"). The speaker refuses to be identified, in any manner, with the life of the married woman.

Instead of the symbols of wedded life, the poet proposes images of self-sufficiency and self-expression. The cold, harsh beauty of a frosted leaf, suggesting danger and exposure to the elements, supplants the sluggish tranquillity of the snail. The open cauldron of self-expression replaces the enclosed tin of repression. The poet embraces the aloneness of the Alps as opposed to the shared life of marriage. Finally, the image of shattered reflections, as in the broken surface of the sea, takes the place of the smooth mirror of the wedding ring that once held the sun's reflection in it. Conflict and violence, in other words, surface from below and destroy the outward calm of marriage.

The final stanza affirms that the poet's true "season" is her love, symbolized by the extreme climatic opposites, cold and heat, frost on a green leaf and fire in the freezing Alps. These are the appropriate images for her love of the self-sufficient, the anomalous, and the unrepressed. Unlike a married woman, the poet will have nothing to do with the season of snails (spring) or with the world of the kitchen. The couriers, which can be thought of as the poems themselves, bring news of the poet's spiritual location and condition on the top of mountains and on the shattered sea surface; her isolation and her love of nature become her source of personal triumph.

"The Couriers" is, like most of the late work, "personal poetry." Its hermetic images constitute a private language of the psyche that at first seem opaque and impenetrable. Yet its rapid association of images and its manipulation of condensed symbolic elements reveals, more accurately than any other technique could, the personal world of conflict and process that the poet experiences. On second and third readings, the poem's metaphors, opposed image sequences, and elliptic development seem the appropriate and natural methods of conveying the tense, deep contradictions involved in marriage and love. The dominant metaphor of the poem—poetry as a courier for imagistic "messages"—indicates that Plath's late poetry is not self-enclosed but is open to the reader as recipient of its message.

Further, the image of the cauldron in "The Couriers" links it to "Ariel," with its "cauldron of morning," and to "Lady Lazarus" and "Fever 103°," with their dominant fire imagery. These poems all imagine a new form of existence for the individual persona. The female speakers throw off an unwanted identity and discover images for their new state: in "The Couriers," the cauldron on the mountain tops; in "Ariel," the arrow and the cauldron; in "Lady Lazarus," the red-haired demon; in "Fever 103°," the Virgin Mary. However, Plath successfully varies the stylistic and imagistic components of these four personal dramas of transformation so that we experience each of these poems as a self-contained aesthetic experience with its persona, action, and imagery. The voices of the speakers are quite different. In "The Couriers," the poetic voice is clipped and somewhat muted; in "Ariel," it is fluent and energetic; in "Lady Lazarus," it turns shrill and hysterical; and in "Fever 103°," it becomes meditative and whimsical. We may, of course, link all the speakers to Plath herself and view the various dramas as autobiographical reflections, but this is hardly necessary. The poems embody an objective pattern: the movement from the familiar world of stasis and death to a new universe of life and energy.

The late poems specifically about marriage and the family take up the same issue as does "The Couriers." They show a woman who either is trapped in her family situation or attempts to escape from that situation. The image of woman's condition is identical in Plath's poetry to the condition of mankind as a whole. "The Jailor," for example, goes even further than "The Couriers" in its negative representation of marriage. Marriage is a form of imprisonment, an identification confirmed in several other works. In this extraordinary dramatization of female victimization and suffering, Plath equates the woman's entrapment to the victimization of all men by a hostile universe. Its nine five-line stanzas present increasingly intense images of physical torture inflicted upon the female speaker by her "jailor." This fantasized relation between prisoner and jailor clearly reflects the sado-masochism of a husband-wife relation. The poem describes the woman's sleeping with her jailor, his sexual abuse of her, her addiction to pills ("red and blue zeppelins" that lift her to the sky), his dependence upon her for security, and, finally, his jealousy of any diversion of her attention from him. The central theme of the poem is, in fact, the male jailor's need for his victim, whom he rapes, starves, burns, and humiliates: " . . . what would he / Do, do, do without me?" This sado-masochism recalls "Daddy," where the father-husband figure is a Nazi torturer. But in "The Jailor" the woman cannot liberate herself from her sexual-physical imprisonment, as the daughter in "Daddy" can. Plath ends "The Jailor" with a series of cosmic analogies to the sado-masochistic relation, thus implying that the universe is constituted as a mechanism of torture:

> What would the dark
> Do without fevers to eat?
> What would the light
> Do without eyes to knive, what would he
> Do, do, do without me?[2]

Here is a prison of such monumental proportions that the jailors are not men but light and dark, the basic elements of the universe. The human encounter between man and woman, husband and wife, jailor and prisoner becomes identical to the cosmic confrontation between life and death.

The sense of woman's entrapment in marriage also characterizes "The Applicant" and "Purdah," but in "Purdah" the female speaker liberates herself by revolting against her husband. Just as the future bride in "The Applicant" is a convenient domestic helper, the wife in "Purdah" is nothing more than a "doll," a plaything. A traditional woman of the Muslim countries, the veiled speaker refuses to be "The agonized / Side of a green Adam" (*WT*, p. 40). She plans to unleash the lioness from within herself. These images of woman as a domestic slave indicate one side of Plath's vision of marriage. She came to see the transformation of self as a process that must be consummated outside of the relationships of marriage.

Her view of marriage and the family has another aspect, however. In the radio play *Three Women*, a much more positive view of the process of marrying and having children emerges. *Three Women* was written at the beginning of Plath's final creative period. It is a clear and often magnificent description of the threatened and vulnerable identities of women experiencing childbirth. Three speakers—a Wife, a Secretary, and a Girl—talk of their pregnancy, childbirth, and return from the hospital. The Wife has a boy; the Secretary miscarries; and the Girl gives birth to a daughter, whom she gives up for adoption. Since Plath herself had a boy and a girl and suffered a miscarriage, much of *Three Women* inevitably reflects her own feelings about childbirth. The autobiographical origin of the speakers' voices may account for the major difficulty with *Three Women*: Plath's failure adequately to differentiate among the styles and voices of the three speakers. The radio play often sounds as if only one woman were speaking rather than three. Another explanation is that no separate, identifiable actions define the characters of the women; as a result, dramatic character does not and cannot clearly emerge. What happens in *Three Women* happens internally, as in *Ariel* and *Winter Trees*, even though the form of the play demands distinguishing external action.

This objection to the presentational method of *Three Women* does not reflect adversely on the thematic and imagistic skill with which the speakers' situations are developed. The richness of imagistic development should be evident to anyone who reads or listens to the radio play, as should the care with which Plath has organized the various stages of the characters' experience. There are six movements or stages in the play: reminiscences of conception along with anticipation of childbirth; the hospital world before delivery; delivery itself; recovery in the hospital; the moment of departure from the hospital; and, finally, the return home. The imagery used by the women consistently develops Plath's major symbolic elements—moon, sun, child, emptiness, redness, and whiteness. These images serve to unify and to focus the emotional issues involved in the drama, especially inasmuch as each of the women faces identical problems: fear of sterility, female vulnerability, and eventual motherhood. The Girl, for example, almost always accentuates the negative and threatening aspects of childbirth; the delivery room, for example, is "a place of shrieks" (*WT*, p. 52). When she sees her daughter in the nursery, she thinks that the child's mouth "cannot be good" (p. 56). The Girl abandons her daughter, attempting to put behind her the awful memory of conception and childbirth, but her effort to deny motherhood only makes her feel intensely sterile and empty, a feeling that is common to all the

women at different moments. Flatness, whiteness, and empti-
ness are the images that repeatedly objectify this mood: the
"flatness" of doctors and of the moon (p. 52); the "winter of
white sheets" in the hospital that portends death to red, living
flowers (p. 59); the "white clean chamber with its instruments"
(p. 52); and the "emptiness" that suddenly appears in the Girl's
room as she is about to leave her daughter forever (p. 59). The
Girl's recovery from her loss is hardly complete.

Like the Girl, the Secretary experiences a loss; but she
reacts differently to every aspect of the childbirth. She is
passionately hostile toward men. Men are "flat," that is, infer-
tile, cold, noncompassionate. For her the issues of gender
reduce to one issue: women's fertility versus men's sterility.
Women are round, red, growing, and alive; men are flat,
white, abstract, and dead. With this polarized conception, it is
no surprise that the Secretary feels that her entire identity as a
woman has been destroyed when she miscarries. Her seven
monologues trace the course of her depression as she increas-
ingly condemns herself for being like men, flat and sterile.

In the first of her monologues she sees "death in the bare
trees," a repeated image, and feels empty among the "flat" men
at the office. The second describes the "white world of snow"
in the hospital, again insisting on the flatness of men, their
hostility to women, and the hatred of the male God for all
people. The monologue in the delivery room imagines that a
hideous earth-mother will devour all mankind because "men
have used her meanly" (p. 54). After delivery, she feels as if the
moon's rays have entered her and made her sterile: "I am
helpless as the sea at the end of her string [the moon's]. / I am
restless. Restless and useless. I, too, create corpses" (p. 55).
This feeling culminates in her assertion that she has lost her
sexual identity: "Neither a woman, happy to be like a man,
nor a man / Blunt and flat enough to feel no lack. I feel a lack"
(p. 55). In the fifth and sixth monologues she has herself
become flat like men: "I am flat and virginal" (p. 59). Her
sense of sterility expresses itself in her perceptions of na-

ture as infertile; thus, as she leaves the hospital, she comments on some twigs: "These little black twigs do not think to bud, / Nor do these dry, dry gutters dream of rain" (pp. 59–60). Like the Girl, she returns home to overcome the shattering of her identity. Her final lines, though, present an image of natural fertility, of growing grass, which implies hope and new life for her.

The Wife's story provides a normative contrast with the other two women's disasters. Although she suffers the same agonies as they through childbirth, she is more positive than they, both before and after delivery. Her first monologue mentions her "astonishment at fertility"; she compares herself to a pheasant showing off her feathers on a hill, as the sun and stars watch her. Her anticipatory fears of childbirth are intense (second monologue), but again certain images of fertility alter the context of physical suffering: "I am dumb and brown, I am a seed about to break. / The brownness is my dead self" (p. 51). The symbolism of rebirth thus appears in her monologue in the midst of pain. Her speech during delivery insists on horrifying images of horses, blackness, and trees; but her fourth monologue immediately turns to images of growth: the red lotus is in bloom, lilies are like the lids of her child. Similarly, the address to her son is positive, praising his beauty, innocence, and purity (fifth monologue). She admits in the sixth monologue that she fears for her son; his vulnerability upsets her. Yet when she returns home, she realizes that he forms part of the cycle of natural growth. Again, flowers symbolize hope and life for her. She ends by affirming what neither of the other speakers could affirm, her child's independence from herself; and she assures him that he will be free to grow and "to marry what he wants and where he will" (p. 62).

The central elements of *Three Women*—the opposition between fertility and sterility in women, the hatred for men, the ambivalence toward children—achieve a resolution in the play that is structurally identical to that of the initiatory dramas. The visit to the hospital, the ordeal of childbirth, and the return home form a three-stage journey to rebirth. Paralleling the purely symbolic rebirth of "Lady Lazarus," the childbirth scenes of *Three Women* bring the initiatory theme onto a realistic plane. The radio play provides a dramatic presentation of the ritual process in "The Stones" or "Ariel."

The relationship of mother and child, which is so important in *Three Women*, takes on great significance in the lyrics.[3] The ambivalence toward children in *Three Women* gives way almost exclusively to the idealization of childhood purity. Plath uses the baby and the child as symbols of the strength and freshness that she herself wishes to possess. The initiatory character of these poems emerges in the light of Plath's recurrent imagery of regression and rebirth in the dramas of initiation. The child embodies traits of exuberance, natural spontaneity, and freshness that a poem like "The Stones" had imagined for the self.

Animal metaphors appear in several of the poems about children: the child as an eel ("You're"); as a cat ("Morning Song"); as a hedgehog ("By Candlelight"). The closeness of the child to animal origins in turn gives him or her a greater natural grace and spontaneity. In "The Night Dances," Nick engages in "pure leaps and spirals" (*A*, p. 17); in "You're," he is "Jumpy as a Mexican bean" (*A*, p. 52); and in "Magi," Frieda "rocks on all fours like a padded hammock" (*CW*, p. 26). What seems to be most attractive to Plath about the child's condition is a clarity of consciousness unspoiled by adult fears and imaginings. This contrast is the point of "For a Fatherless Son," in which the mother loves the "stupidity" of her son because his "blind mirror" reflects only her face, not the inner landscape of her mind: "The small skulls, the smashed blue hills, the godawful hush" (*WT*, p. 33). Throughout these poems, the image of the blank slate or tabula rasa recurs most frequently as either a quality of the child's mind or an aspect of the world he or she perceives. In "You're," Nick is a "clean slate" (p. 52); in "Child," his "clear eye" is the "one absolutely beautiful thing" (*WT*, p. 18); in "Brasília," he is a "mirror" (*WT*, p. 11); and in "Morning Song," he is also a "mirror" (*A*,

p. 1). The adjectives "clear," "clean," and "pure" apply frequently to the child as signs of the innocence that Plath values above everything in the world.

The forces of death that can potentially destroy this innocence are well dramatized in "Nick and the Candlestick." In the first seven stanzas the poet imagines the child's cold room as a frozen, icicle-filled cave and herself as a miner carrying a blue light. The images suggest a world of death in which all familiar objects have been transformed into hostile ones. Two or three readings may be required to realize that all the objects in the room have been internalized and transformed by the poet before she describes them. The metaphorical cave seems at first to be an actual cave, but it is not. The piranha in the cave are actually fish in a bowl or aquarium, but Plath says they form "A piranha / Religion, drinking / Its first communion out of my live toes" (*A*, p. 33). The "calcium icicles," the white newts, a flickering candle, and the coldness all appear to be absolutely real until the eighth stanza, when the poem suddenly breaks the mood with a direct address to the baby, and we realize that the poem takes place in the baby's room:

> O love, how did you get here?
> O embryo
>
> Remembering, even in sleep,
> Your crossed position.
> The blood blooms clean
>
> In you, ruby.
> The pain
> You wake to is not yours.
>
> [pp. 33–34]

The child is completely oblivious to the mother's world of cosmic oppression and hostility, of freezing cold and natural danger. Sleeping as if still in the protected womb, the baby is ironically more "solid" than the mother because he is unaffected by the terrible vision that visits her. The baby is "the one / Solid the spaces lean on." The paradoxical invulnerability of the child leads the poet to affirm his Christlike power in the face of the world's destructive forces, symbolized by the stars falling into blackness and "the mercuric / Atoms that cripple" dripping "Into the terrible well." The poem culminates in the mother's affirmation of faith in the idealized child; she calls him "the baby in the barn."

The brilliance of "Nick and the Candlestick" lies in its simple modulation from color imagery to the imagery of Christ. The first seven stanzas establish the white world of death, the cave, and its dangerous animals. The next four stanzas shift to the redness of the baby, with references to "blood," "ruby," and "roses." Redness stands for the warmth and beauty of the life force, as almost always in the late poems. And the final three stanzas reintroduce the death motif through the symbolism of blackness, only to end in the final image of the Christ child in the barn. The poem moves effortlessly from the imaginary environment of the cave to the real world of the room and, finally, to the mythical reality of the manger. It is a beautiful balancing of the horrors and joys of Plath's inner world.

The polarity between the child's purity and the world's hostility appears in most of the poems about children, though not usually with the brilliance of "Nick and the Candlestick." In "Magi" the visiting kings offer the child a blanched, abstracted version of life, intellectualized beyond all relation to her exuberant and miraculous bodily existence. "The Night Dances" pictures the "black amnesias of heaven" in contrast to the human gestures of the child prancing in the crib. In both poems the negative forces of the universe, whether they are intellectual or physical, oppose the perfect spontaneity and vitality of the child. Similarly, "Child" sets the blackness of the sky over against the hope and joy of the child. "Thalidomide" is the monologue of a mother who has had a normal child and thus been spared the horror of "dark / Amputations" (*WT*, p. 23). Finally, "Brasília" makes this opposition strongest when the mother prays:

O You who eat

People like light rays, leave
this one
Mirror safe, unredeemed

By the dove's annihilation,
The glory
The power, the glory.

[*WT*, pp. 11–12]

This "reverse" prayer, a prayer *against* redemption, sets the
innocence and beauty of the child against the traditional vision
of the Holy Ghost, according to which man's evil must be
purged through the visitation of death and destruction. For
Plath, God is the destructive power in the universe, who may
take away the one purely good, spontaneous, unspoiled crea-
ture she knows: her baby. *From* God's power, then, Plath
prays to be delivered. She wishes only to be with her child,
who is her vision of Christ.

Of the poems that concentrate on the family, those dealing
with the father provide the clearest and most powerful example
of Plath's divided conception of the universe. "Daddy" (1962)
is, of course, Plath's most important poem on the theme of the
family, but it expresses only one-half of her poetic treatment of
the father image. In the earlier poetry, the father appears in an
idealized form; by the time of "Daddy," he embodies all the
traits of oppressiveness and authoritarianism that Plath drama-
tizes in the Nazi doctor in "Lady Lazarus." The development
of the patriarchal figure in the poems varies a pattern that
charactrized the landscapes and seascapes: the later poetry
personalizes the concerns of the early work by specifying in
detail the poet's death-and-life drama. The poems about the
father demonstrate Plath's ability to convert private psychic
material—fantasies, memories, family history—into coherent
dramatic forms.

The first poem on the family theme is "Lament" (1951–52),

which praises the father's heroism; the title of Plath's first book, of course, refers to him symbolically. Seven poems directly mention the father, and many more deal with the complex of images and ideas attached to his memory: the Giant, the Colossus, or the Black Man, who controls reality for good or for evil. The poems describe the progressive modification and eventual denial of childhood idealizations of him as heroic, omnipotent, and good. "Lament" keeps intact the shape of the ideal father and retains what must be an early explanation of how he died. The premise of the villanelle is that the heroic father was killed by the "sting of bees" (*CG*, p. 27).

In "On the Decline of Oracles," written while Plath was at Cambridge (1956–57), she makes clear that the loss of the father destroyed the daughter's sense of the heroic possibilities of life, making everyone alive seem trivial and unimportant.[4] The title of the poem is derived from a painting by Giorgio de Chirico ("L'Enigme de l'Oracle"), and the poem's epigraph is by de Chirico as well: "Inside a ruined temple the broken statue of a god speaks a mysterious language."[5] The oracle is, of course, another version of the Colossus. Like the giant statue, the oracle has "declined," that is, it fails to make sense when it speaks. Alluding to the heroic world of Greece, the poet claims that she once "descried Troy's towers fall, / Saw evil break out of the north," referring to the calamity of her father's death.

Although the division between father and external world appears to be a simple opposition between the protecting parent and the dangerous, unknown environment, it conceals a powerful contradiction. If her father died, then the daughter's view of his awesome power must be exaggerated. One way out of this contradiction, which strikes at the basis of her idealization, is rebirth, as dramatized in "Full Fathom Five." Taking her title from *The Tempest* (I. 2. 387), "Full fathom five thy father lies," Plath locates him alive under the sea. She presents him as the traditional patriarch, "white hair, white beard, far flung" (*C*, 46). He controls a kingdom under water, and she hopes to rejoin him below. Another possible way out of the contradiction is the father's resurrection. Although this possibility is finally negated in "The Colossus," the poem dramatizes a version of the Pygmalion story: the daughter wishes to bring her father's statue back to life. Similarly, "The Beekeeper's Daughter" reflects on the father's lost power without the daughter being able to resurrect him. Death and fertility are intertwined; the queen bee has what "no mother can contest— / A fruit that's death to taste: dark flesh, dark parings" (*C*, p. 73). And as the daughter bends down to look at the queen bee in her hive, she fantasizes that her father, "The bridegroom," has married the queen. In the apiary in which her father spent so much time, Plath is undoubtedly identifying with the object of his attention, the bee.

The image of the "evil" father in "Daddy" is foreshadowed in two poems from 1956, "Complaint of the Crazed Queen" and "The Snowman on the Moor." Because the images in these works are so similar to images associated with the father in other poems—whiteness, deathlike appearance, gigantic size, sudden disappearance—there is little doubt that Plath is projecting an alternative vision of the father. In both poems a giant threatens and oppresses women. He is not a heroic patriarch but an aggressive marauder, and yet the women ultimately find the giant either persuasive or attractive. They come to recognize the virtue in obedience to gigantic men.

Two other poems indicate a change in another aspect of the idealization, showing that the father will not return from the grave to help the daughter. "November Graveyard" is about the father's grave, deriving its title from the fact that Plath's father died in November of 1940. The poem argues that elegiac conventions of natural renewal and religious conventions of resurrection lose their power in the face of "one stark skeleton," that is, the father's skeleton.[6] "Ouija" symbolizes the father in the form of a god of shades, who "Rises to the glass from his black fathoms" (*CW*, p. 44). The father-god is in love with the "bawdy queen of death" and wants only to write florid poetic praises of death's beauty. "Ouija" thus states the daughter's unhappy realization that the father is married not to her but to his own deathly queen.

The most revealing early poem on the father is "Electra on Azalea Path" (1958). It summarizes the forms of idealization in the previous work, but introduces a new psychic element: the daughter admits to an enormous sense of guilt for having loved the father. The form of this admission is a fantasy based on the story of Electra. The Electra persona imagines that her incestuous love for the father was reciprocated and that he committed suicide out of guilt for his attraction to her. The ultimate object of this revision of family history is to implicate Plath in her father's death, thus making them both actors in a tragedy of forbidden love: "I brought my love to bear, and then you died"; "I am the ghost of an infamous suicide."[7] By connecting her love and the father's natural death, she both enjoys the fantasy of having won the father away from her mother and punishes herself for it.

"Electra on Azalea Path" dramatizes the dead father as Agamemnon, the mother as Clytemnestra, and the daughter as a guilt-ridden Electra. Its revelation of guilt and sexuality eventually leads to a new image of the father as the Black Man and the daughter as his victim.[8] "Little Fugue," written at the end of 1961, abandons the image of the heroic Greek father and denies that the daughter should feel guilty. The father is black, authoritarian, and Germanic. The daughter, faced with a negative image, can declare: "I am guilty of nothing" (*A*, p. 71). She now presents her father through the image of a black yew tree:

> I see your voice
> Black and leafy, as in my childhood,
>
> A yew hedge of orders,
> Gothic and barbarous, pure German.
> Dead men cry from it.

> [*A*, pp. 70–71]

The desolate image of the yew tree, later developed in "The Moon and the Yew Tree," is antithetical to the earlier image of the white, stonelike patriarch, since the yew tree is organic and thus mortal. Furthermore, the blackness of the yew image indicates a hidden viciousness in the father, a sadism that becomes obvious in "Daddy." The daughter is obsessed with images of dismemberment and cutting when she thinks of him:

> And you, during the Great War
> In the California delicatessen
>
> Lopping the sausages!
> They colour my sleep,
> Red, mottled, like cut necks.
> There was a silence!
>
> [*A*, p. 71]

Yet "Little Fugue" ultimately does not stress the father's authoritarianism and dangerousness as much as his vulnerability and helplessness. He has one leg because Otto Plath's left leg was amputated before he died; and when death comes to swallow him in its black tree, it leaves only a black silence, which frightens the daughter. Plath symbolizes this aspect of death in "The Munich Mannequins" through the image of black telephones on hooks, "Glittering and digesting / Voicelessness" (*A*, p. 74). The yew tree may once have issued orders, but now the fingers of the mute yew motion to the clouds and are ignored. In the same way, the silent father has lost his powers of communication, leaving his daughter bereft and unconsoled.

Images of blackness and Germanic harshness eventually supplant the earlier complex of images relating to the father. Plath completely reverses the idealization of the father, profoundly changing the character of her late work and her treatment of death. The vicious, unmerciful father is now the equivalent in the family world of the brutal Nazis in the historical world. Blackness is the key imagistic element indicating the presence of the father. He is the Nazi doctor in

"Lady Lazarus," the composite enemy-god-devil who perse-
utes women. He is the priest in cassock and black boots in
"Berck Plage," symbolizing death and cruelty: "This black
boot," says the speaker, "has no mercy for anybody" (*A*, p. 21).
In "The Bee Meeting" he is the rector, a nefarious man in black
("Which is the rector now, is it that man in black?") [*A*, p. 56]
who leads the villagers in frightening bee-rites. In "Years" he is
God, with his unresponsive "black void"; and in "Daddy" he is
the father-husband who brutalizes the daughter.

"Daddy" is, of course, Plath's most extended treatment of
the father symbol, though it is by no means her best poem.
The rapid, often wild succession of elements relating to the
father are not entirely integrated into the poem. It opens with
a reference to the father's black shoe, in which the daughter
has "lived like a foot," suggesting her submissiveness and en-
trapment. The poem then moves to a derisive commentary on
the idealized image of the father ("Marble heavy, a bag full of
God") and summarizes his background: his life in a German-
speaking part of Poland that was "Scraped flat by the roller / Of
wars" (*A*, p. 49). The daughter admits here, for the first time
in the poetry, that she was afraid of him. Yet all these refer-
ences are merely introductory remarks to prepare the reader
for the fantastic "allegory" that is to come. As Plath describes
it in her note: "The poem is spoken by a girl with an Electra
complex. Her father died while she thought he was God. Her
case is complicated by the fact that her father was also a Nazi
and her mother very possibly part Jewish. In the daughter the
two strains marry and paralyze each other—she has to act out
the awful little allegory once before she is free of it."[9]

The plot of "Daddy" is almost completely invented. Plath's
real father was not a Nazi, and her mother was not Jewish.
The historical references, however, allow her to dramatize her
rebellion against the oppressive father. The entire poem may
seem to have stretched the permissible limits of analogy. This
piece of "light verse," as Plath called it, constantly shifts be-
tween grotesque, childish flights and allusions and deadly

serious rage toward the father-Nazi.[10] On one hand, Plath characterizes her situation in terms of nursery rhymes, recalling the tale of the old lady in the shoe; and on the other, of Jews being taken off to "Dachau, Auschwitz, Belsen" (p. 50). The father is a "Panzer-man," but he is also called "gobbledygoo." German and English intermix grotesquely:

> I never could talk to you.
> The tongue stuck in my jaw.
>
> It stuck in a barb wire snare.
> Ich, ich, ich, ich.
>
> [p. 49]

There is a line as startling and compact as this: "Every woman adores a Fascist"; but there is also the fatuousness of the lines following: "The boot in the face, the brute / Brute heart of a brute like you" (p. 50). And the end of the poem drops the carefully established Nazi allegory for a piece of vampire lore. Plath imagines that a vampire-husband has impersonated the dead Nazi-father for seven years of marriage, drinking the wife's blood, until she has finally put a stake through his heart (the traditional method of destroying the vampire).

"Daddy" is obviously an attempt to do away altogether with the idealized father; but it also makes clear how difficult a task that is. Daddy keeps returning in the poem in different guises: statue, shoe, Nazi, teacher, devil, and vampire. If the starting point of Plath's idealization of the father was the heroic white patriarch of "Lament," the end point is the black vampire of "Daddy." The father has been reenvisioned in terms of his sexual dominance, cruelty, and authoritarianism. Ironically, the father, who was mourned in the earlier poems as the innocent victim of deathly external forces, has himself been transformed into the agent of death. It is as if the underside of Plath's feelings toward the father had surfaced, abolishing the entire "epic," that she described in "Electra on Azalea Path" and replacing it with a new cast of characters and a new plot. The story is no longer the daughter's attempt to reunite with and to marry the dead father; it is now the daughter's wish to overthrow his dominance over her imagination and to "kill" him and the man who takes his place—the vampire in "Daddy," the Nazi in "Lady Lazarus," or the husband in "Purdah." Rebellion and anger supplant the grief and depression of the earlier poems.

The link between the father's death, the family theme, and the theme of death is crucial to the development of Plath's poetry as a whole. The entire sequence of images in *The Colossus* involving stone, water, statuary, and death took on their character of despair and mourning from their association with the Greek "epic" of the father. The Greek stage of idealization involved a stark contrast between the self and the distant, unconcerned, hostile world. Everything in life seemed a trivialization, a fall, from the original relation that childhood had established to the great father, to the sea, to the natural world, and to language and art. But the later work progressively undermines the illusion of ideal paternity; a greater consciousness of the sexuality of the daughter's relation to the father and of the father's authoritarian ways surface. The poet now identifies herself as the victim of men in general, of the father figure in particular, and sees the whole world in terms of a brutal battle for dominance between life and death. As in "The Jailor," death is the one fact that governs all of reality. Plath no longer feels protected by the father from the external world; he is as murderous as God or predatory animals. The only kinship that Plath feels is with the life force carving its way through the blackness—with the red poppies, the beautiful fertile trees, or the innocent children. Blackness, the fundamental color of death in the late poems, is the color shared by the Black Man and all his related symbols—the yew tree, the black telephone, the black boots, the vampire, and the black sky into which all things human and nonhuman vanish.

Two groups of late poems explore the poet's relationship to women and to nature. "The Rival," "The Rival (2)," "Medusa,"

"The Other," and "Lesbos" are all dramatic monologues attacking women who threaten the speaker's individuality. In the first three of these poems the Rival and the Medusa represent negative versions of the mother. In "The Rival," the Rival appears as the omnipresent, hostile moon, an image that is always associated with the mother in Plath's work. Like the Medusa, she has the ability to turn the world to stone: she haunts the poet by constantly observing her from a distance. Similarly, "The Rival (2)" imagines that the Rival has an "eye" that perpetually gazes at the speaker and refuses to leave her alone. The Rival's hostile form is even found washed up on the beach, "with the sound of the sea in your mouth" (*P*, p. 8). "Medusa" paints the portrait of a similar figure: she observes the speaker from across the Atlantic; she has a hideous head that can apparently turn the self to stone; and she wishes to hurt the speaker. The reference in the poem to the umbilical attachment between the poet and Medusa identifies this figure as the mother. Plath also alludes to a visit that her mother made to England in the summer of 1962 in the line: "You steamed to me over the sea." Unlike the Rival poems, however, "Medusa" attempts to cast off the parental image and to attain personal independence. "Medusa" corresponds in Plath's work to "Daddy": both represent the search for freedom from parental figures.

Whereas these three poems are directed at the negative image of Plath's mother, "The Other" and "Lesbos" refer to figures from Plath's life in England. "The Other" alludes to the mistress of Plath's husband, and "Lesbos" deals with an incident that occurred at a friend's house while Plath was living in Devon.[11] Both poems suffer, however, from glaring defects. "Lesbos" expresses Plath's hatred for a neighbor who had forced Plath's daughter to leave her kittens outside the house when they visited; the intensity of vilification and hate in the poem hardly seems warranted by the incident. "The Other" is simply too obscure a poem to work effectively. Dramatic monologues cannot succeed unless they establish a comprehensible dramatic frame, as Plath does in "The Applicant." "The Other" jumps from private image to private image without clarifying for the reader their meaning; it remains impenetrable. The same fault mars such late poems as "The Secret" and "The Fearful," which also relate to Plath's feelings about her separation from her husband.

Of the late poems about nature, the most famous are the bee poems: "The Bee Meeting," "The Arrival of the Bee Box," "Stings," "Stings (2)," "The Swarm," and "Wintering." Plath uses the bees as metaphors for a number of different concerns. In "The Bee Meeting" the ceremony of moving the queen allows her to identify with the apparently victimized hive. She herself feels threatened; and the Gothic horror of veiled bee gatherers who have come for the queen dramatizes her participation in a death ritual. "The Arrival of the Bee Box" approaches the ritual of death from the opposite angle: now the poet controls the bees rather than identifying with them, and her reaction is one of guilt for entrapping them and horror at their dangerousness. The bees seem to her to be deformed creatures, tainted with death. Her only escape is to promise that their "box is only temporary" (*A*, p. 60).

"Stings" and "Stings (2)" both relate to an incident that took place in June 1962. Bees attacked Plath's husband, who was unprotected by veils, while Plath was moving the queen. These poems stress the revenge of the bees against those who disturb their hives. The queen, for instance, ascends above the world in much the same way that Lady Lazarus ascends:

> Now she is flying
> More terrible than she ever was, red
> Star in the sky, red comet
> Over the engine that killed her—
> The mausoleum, the wax house.

[*A*, p. 63]

Whereas "The Bee Meeting" and "The Arrival of the Bee Box" focused on the ritual of domination and victimization in

the natural world, "Stings" and "Stings (2)" use this particular
incident as a veiled reference to Plath's own feelings of revenge
against her husband and as a metaphor for personal violence.
The bee metaphor has thus widened to encompass the poet's
relationship to her family.

In the final two poems of the series, the metaphor takes on
political and personal dimensions. "The Swarm" establishes a
parallel between the shooting of the swarm and the defeat of
Napoleon at Waterloo. The point of the poem is that the
murders of history are much like the violence men commit
against the natural world. The poet's identification with the
victims produces momentary flashes of brilliance ("The gilt
and pink domes of Russia melt and float off"), but the work as
a whole is too long and diffuse. "Wintering" culminates the
series by stressing the complete identification of the poet and
the bees. Looking at the bees who winter inside her wine
cellar, Plath imagines that they occupy the dark center of
reality:

> This is the room I have never been in.
> This is the room I could never breathe in.
> The black bunched in there like a bat,
> No light
> But the torch and its faint
>
> Chinese yellow on appalling objects—
> Black asininity. Decay.

[A, p. 67]

The blackness of the bees in the dead of winter symbolizes
for Plath the organic zero point from which new life will
emerge. From this center where the poet feels possessed by the
bees ("It is they who own me"), she sees an exit. The bees
represent a feminine force that will come out from the long
white winter and be reborn: "The bees are flying. They taste
the spring." Like Plath's other long sequence, "Poem for a
Birthday," the bee sequence ends on a note of reemergent life
after the experiences of ritual, familial, and political death.

The finest poems of Plath's last period refine and concentrate the vision of death and life in the bee sequence. A list of her best poems would have to include "Ariel," "Fever 103°," "Lady Lazarus," "A Birthday Present," "Death & Co.," "Totem," and "The Munich Mannequins." These poems integrate the elements of the earlier work—woman's situation, nature, the family—into every aspect of the imagistic structure. "Ariel" is probably Plath's finest single construction because of the precision and depth of its images. In its account of the ritual journey toward the center of life and death, Plath perfects her method of leaping from image to image in order to represent mental process. The sensuousness and concreteness of the poem—the "Black sweet blood mouthfuls" of the berries; the "glitter of seas"—is unmatched in contemporary American poetry. We see, hear, touch, and taste the process of disintegration: the horse emerging from the darkness of the morning, the sun beginning to rise as Ariel rushes uncontrollably across the countryside, the rider trying to catch the brown neck but instead "tasting" the blackberries on the side of the road. Then all the rider's perceptions are thrown together: the horse's body and the rider's merge. She hears her own cry as if it were that of a child and flies toward the burning sun that has now risen.

In "Ariel," Plath finds a perfect blend between Latinate and colloquial dictions, between abstractness and concreteness. The languages of her earlier and her later work come together:

> White
> Godiva, I unpeel—
> Dead hands, dead stringencies.

> [*A*, p. 26]

The concreteness of the Anglo-Saxon "hands" gives way to the abstractness of the Latinate "stringencies": both the physical and psychological aspects of the self have died and are pared away. Finally, the treatment of aural effects in the poem makes it the finest of Plath's technical accomplishments. The slant-rhymes, the assonance (for example, the "I"-sound in the last three stanzas), and the flexible three-line stanzas provide a superb music.

"Fever 103°" and "Lady Lazarus" are Plath's two finest dramatic monologues. "Fever 103°" is the better poem because of its subtler modulations of tone and its greater variety of images. Personal perspectives on the speaker's sense of sin and her self-punishment merge effortlessly with cosmic views of death and historical considerations of Hiroshima. The dramatic monologue provides a form for the speaker's quick shifts of perception and address. At the beginning of the poem, she appears to be answering her own internal question about self-purification through suffering ("Pure? What does it mean?"); in the middle of the poem, she turns to her husband and resolves her doubts ("I am too pure for you or anyone"); and at the end, she transforms herself into a "pure acetylene / Virgin," who can reject all attachments to others. The speaker is aware, however, of her own fantastic imaginative leaps: the metaphoric flights are gaudy and self-conscious. She thinks that her head has become a Japanese paper-light globe and that her skin has been beaten and expanded as gold is expanded through beating. These physical transformations of the body can be opposed to the more violent self-transformation of "Lady Lazarus." "Fever 103°" moves effortlessly through a great range of positive and negative possibilities for the self: from Isadora Duncan to Hiroshima, from the Virgin to "whore petticoats." At once immersed in the nightmare of radiation poisoning and in a fantasy of religious salvation, the poem gives the most balanced version of Plath's striving toward a purification of self in the midst of the world of death.

A striking contrast to "Fever 103°" is "A Birthday Present," another dramatic monologue in which terror and hysterical panic predominate. The long, two-lined stanzas focus obsessively on the birthday present brought to the speaker by a friend. The speaker, her friend, and the object "talk" to each other in the kitchen. As the speaker attempts to imagine what is behind the veil, she defines it successively as a person, bones, a pearl button, and an ivory tusk. Each of these identifications hints at the nature of the birthday present that she wants. The animate present itself mysteriously asks whether the woman is "the one for the annunciation," not clarifying what that annunciation is (*A*, p. 42). The three white objects— bones, pearl, and ivory tusk—all suggest death because they were once part of living organisms. But the persona only completely explains what she wants as a birthday present when she speaks of the veils around the present. Life itself, she says, is a veil concealing death. In order to remove the concealing veil, which causes her anxiety and fear, the speaker demands an end to the screening off of death from view. By rejecting the "veil" that keeps death at a distance from human consciousness, she hopes to attain a state of nonself-consciousness, of pure self-transcendence. In an extraordinary metaphor toward the end of the poem, she compares her life to the arrival by mail of parts of her own corpse. The delivery, however, is stretched out over the span of sixty years until her entire body is dead: "Let it not," she prays, "come by mail, finger by finger." In the conclusion to the poem, the speaker demands as her birthday present not the previously mentioned symbols of death nor the figure representing death, but death itself:

> If it [the present] were death
>
> I would admire the deep gravity of it, its timeless eyes.
> I would know you were serious.
>
> There would be a nobility then, there would be a birthday.
> And the knife not carve, but enter
>
> Pure and clean as the cry of a baby,
> And the universe slide from my side.

> [p. 44]

The conditional mood of the verbs in this passage—"I *would* admire," "I *would* know"—demonstrates that the persona knows the impossibility of her conception at the very moment that she entertains it. The whole poem dramatizes the ironic vision of this passage; her birthday becomes her death-day, and death becomes a form of rebirth, "Pure and clean as a baby." Only the absoluteness of a knifing, reducing her to the nonself-conscious state of a baby screaming, can be grave enough or noble enough to be a true "birthday" present. As in "Lady Lazarus," the baby's cry is Plath's recurrent image for the self reborn from the disintegrated adult body.

The drama of "A Birthday Present" is frightening in its transformation of a domestic, and usually happy, occasion—the visit of a friend carrying a birthday gift—into a celebration of suicide. It captures the movement of the speaker's mind as she throws herself into the sequence of steps that might lead her to kill herself. Although some critics may claim that without knowledge of Plath's own suicide the poem would lose its "realism," this view denies the great effectiveness of the images and structure of the poem. It presents a coherent dramatic situation that contains within itself all we need to know about the characters and their actions. The projection of the speaker's death fantasies onto the veiled object gives dramatic status to what might be, in the hands of a lesser poet, the confessions of a desperate, suicidal woman. Plath has found a way to create a mysterious and brilliant drama out of her own solitary imaginings of self-destruction.

Like "A Birthday Present," "Death & Co." converts an ordinary human encounter into a metaphor for death. Visited in her hospital bed by two acquaintances, the speaker envisions them as the two faces of death. Plath gives new energy to the old convention of the visit of death in this poem, although she finds no saving religious vision at the end. The two human figures destroy life in different ways.

The first figure is literally voracious and icy; he "eats" people: "I am red meat. His beak / Claps sidewise . . ." (*A*, p. 28). The second uses people in order to be loved; he is a pure narcissist: "Bastard / Masturbating a glitter, . . ." Both the voracious and the seductive sides of death appear to the speaker in a kind of vision; she simply notes their existence, as if it were "perfectly natural." The poem ends, however, with another brilliant vision that stresses the purely natural and automatic processes of death:

> I do not stir.
> The frost makes a flower,
> The dew makes a star,
> The dead bell,
> The dead bell.
>
> Somebody's done for.
>
> [pp. 28–29]

Death is as common and daily an occurrence as the dew on the grass or the frost on a window pane; it is as beautiful and as icy as the latter. "Death & Co." is thus one of Plath's extended metaphors for the reality of death. It is not, as A. Alvarez would have it, a poem of suicide.[12]

Two of Plath's most vivid presentations of the world of death were written within the last month of her life. "The Munich Mannequins" and "Totem," both written in January 1963, confront the dead void of space. "The Munich Mannequins" makes a complex metaphoric equation between the external snowy night, which brings whiteness and cold to the earth, and the naked, bald mannequins in a shop window in Munich, which symbolize the perfection and sterility of death. Set against the silence and mindlessness of the snow and the mannequins is the human procreative urge and the generational cycle: "The blood flood is the flood of love, / The absolute sacrifice" (*A*, p. 73). Human life will never cease releasing new seeds and eggs, imaged as "moons," but the death world is already perfected and has no need to grow. Blood therefore encounters the perfection of death all around it: in the silence of the white snow, in the baldness of the mannequins, in the horror of German history, and in the voicelessness of black, unused telephones. Plath finds an absolute loneliness and isolation for the human being in the universe.

"Totem" is an even more intense statement of the primordial relation between blood and death. In its two central lines, Plath writes: "The world is blood-hot and personal / Dawn says, with its blood-flush" (*A*, pp. 75–76). The poem gives ample evidence to support this statement: the blood of pigs slaughtered by farmers, of hares "Flayed of their fur and humanity," and of human beings "eaten" by death. The vision in "Totem" is of a continuous devouring of the universe by death, an ingestion of people, animals, and even objects (railroad tracks "eaten" by the train). The final images of the poem deny that the train of life can ever find a "terminus." Plath perceives all organic life as flies eaten by a giant spider, an almost Jacobean vision of horror:

I am mad, calls the spider, waving its many arms.

And in truth, it is terrible,
Multiplied in the eyes of the flies.

They buzz like blue children
In nets of the infinite,

Roped in at the end by the one
Death with its many sticks.

[p. 76]

The "totem" of the title, then, is the spider. In its portrayal of a cosmic voraciousness, the poem provides the clearest rendering of Plath's agony in the face of a cannibalistic universe. Appropriately, the poem is filled with animals: pigs, hares, snakes, cobras, flies, and spiders play a role in this devouring universe. Human symbols of spiritual achievement and love, Plato and Christ, are derisively regarded as impotent heads on sticks; they, too, will be eaten. The metaphor of the train ride, which opens and closes the poem, recalls the train ride of "Getting There"; but in this case no redeeming self-transformation occurs to the speaker. Rather than reaching the "terminus" of rebirth, the self simply continues to unfold from suitcases like a suit full of old papers and tickets. The image of old papers and tickets suggests, of course, the self's inability to be reborn.

The closing metaphor of "Totem" indicates the hopelessness of the human situation in a death world. Human beings are flies caught in "nets of the infinite," and their "eyes" (with a pun on "I") always reflect the spider of death. Ritualistic elements predominate in the poem—the eating-chain, the slaughter of the hares, the movement of the train toward a terminus—but the ritual ends in nothingness.

"Totem" reflects the mood of Plath's final months, a mood of despondency and hopelessness that produced a number of extraordinary poems. The initiatory pattern that had been elaborately worked out in the finest work, however, could no longer be maintained. In "Paralytic," for example, the first stages of the initiatory descent are dramatized without an eventual upsurge of life energy. A man connected to an iron lung lies in his hospital bed meditating on his physical condition, his family, and his psychic state. His journey into his past recalls the mental processes of the speaker in "Tulips": both descend into water and blissfully accept the end of their desires and attachments. In "Paralytic," the "still waters / Wrap" the eyes, nose, and ears of the speaker (*A*, p. 78). Inertia and self-absorption replace movement and outward action; the self ends as a kind of "buddha," who no longer desires anything at all from life.

The difference between the vision in "Paralytic" and that in "Tulips," however, could not be clearer: the bedridden persona in "Tulips" emerges from her watery grave-womb to the possibility of new life. The self in "Paralytic" has given up all desire for life. Absorption in death, which had been appealing in such earlier poems as "Full Fathom Five" and "Last Words," now exclusively determimes Plath's vision of the end. In "Poppies in July," "Contusion," "Edge," and "Words," which were written during Plath's last week, initiation has been abandoned in favor of a dramatic play of images leading to incorporation within the earth or water. The poppies in "Poppies in July" symbolize a liquid reality that promises eternal sleep to the poet. Like the water in "Paralytic," they confer complete tranquillity.

"Contusion," "Edge," and "Words" also connect death with absorption and water. As has been previously shown, "Contusion" chillingly describes the body in terms of the purely physical motion of the sea around a rock. The stark metaphors for death—"The sea slides back, / The mirrors are sheeted"—leave no room for hope. "Edge" provides a ritual setting for a suicidal drama. As in the transitional work "Last Words," Plath specifies in this poem the symbolic setting for her death. The Greek imagery of the father poems returns in the description of a dead woman's body draped in the "scrolls of her toga" (*A*, p. 84). Her dead children lie at her breasts; and the death process reverses the process of birth. The children go back *into* the mother's body just as a rose's petals close at night. The mother and children are thus assimilated into nature and the earth in the same way that the self has been absorbed in water in "Paralytic" and "Contusion." The ritual aspect of "Edge," however, is emphasized by the presence of the moon above the woman's body. Like the moon in "The Moon and the Yew Tree" that overlooks the cemetery, this moon observes the dead. Symbolically, the moon is again the mother, "Staring from her hood of bone," indifferent to the death the daughter faces. The death ritual occurs under the eye of an internalized object, a cold mother, who is "used to this sort of thing." Plath has thus envisioned her death in the same landscape and setting that had characterized her poems as far back as *The Colossus*.

The mood of indifference and weariness with life reaches its culmination in "Words," one of Plath's most brilliant but also one of her most despairing statements. The poem shows that Plath maintained a coherent grasp on the technical development of her work until the very end of her life. Plath works out two central metaphoric equations in the poem: language as an ax striking against living trees (the body); language as the echo of the ax stroke riding off like a horse (poetry). The relation between the body and poetry, between death and art, forms the essential subject of "Words." The first part of the poem is energetic and open to emotion:

> Axes
> After whose strokes the wood rings,
> And the echoes!
> Echoes travelling
> Off from the center like horses.
>
> The sap
> Wells like tears, like the
> Water striving
> To re-establish its mirror
> Over the rock
>
> That drops and turns,
> A white skull,
> Eaten by weedy greens.

[A, p. 85]

In the fluid movement from metaphor to metaphor, Plath identifies the white skull thrown into water with the cut made by the ax in the bark of the tree. The water tries to reform its surface after the skull has been dropped into it, just as the sap covers the broken surface of the tree. Metaphorically, then, language introduces death into personal reality, cutting the living body as an ax cuts a tree and as the skull breaks the water's surface. Words damage the original organic wholeness of the body by bringing death into consciousness. The energy of the metaphors in the first part of the poem, however, suggests the power of language to understand death and to face it.

Yet the second part of the poem shows the hopelessness of revitalizing the self through poetry, which is the most intense form of language:

> Years later I
> Encounter them on the road—

Words dry and riderless,
The indefatigable hooftaps.
While
From the bottom of the pool, fixed stars
Govern a life.

Poems are "words" that ride off away from the original act of
thought that gave birth to them. The horse metaphor suggests
"Ariel," with its violent ride toward birth; but these horses are
dry and depersonalized: the poet's self and her language have
been separated from each other. The depersonalization of lan-
guage through writing is, of course, a common experience:
after several years, a piece of writing may no longer be recog-
nizable to its author. Rather than preserving the self, language
may thus make us aware of our distance from ourselves. In
the symbolic terms of "Stillborn," the poems abandon their
mother: "It would be better if they [Plath's poems] were alive,
and that's what they were. / But they are dead, and their
mother near dead with distraction" (*CW*, p. 20).

The final image of "Words" returns to the inward world of
water. Now Plath suggests that an objective factor is operating
within the self and controlling it: "From the bottom of the
pool, fixed stars / Govern a life." The white skull at the water's
bottom has given way to, or been transformed into, the white
stars, a traditional symbol of fate, destiny, or the cosmic order.
Unlike the dissolving and corroding skull, the stars are perma-
nent, unchanging rulers of the poet's life. The poem thus
defines Plath's fundamental sense of doom and fatality; the
hand of the dead rules the living; language cannot overcome
the primordial disturbance created in the self by the conscious-
ness of the dead and death. By presenting these personal
conceptions of language and death in highly elliptical image
sequences, Plath creates a stark but beautiful image of her fate.
It is a personal image, but one that speaks of basic concerns.

Plath's career ends here in a world of death from which
there is no rebirth or transformation. Yet her work, with its
powerful ambivalent use of images and its commitment to

rebirth, dramatizes more than the despairing end game of her final month. The ritual patterns establish themselves in the poems with such force and energy that they provide our most striking sense of Plath's quality as a poet: a woman who could throw herself into the center of death in order to be recalled to life in a different form of existence, the form given her by the poem of transformation.

six _____

Poetry and Suffering

Art for the artist is only suffering through which
he releases himself for further suffering.[1]
—Franz Kafka

No recent body of American poetry has produced as strongly divided a response among its readers as Sylvia Plath's. One obvious reason for the conflicting opinions about her work lies in the sensational extraliterary aspects of her suicide, but a more significant cause for uneasiness can be attributed to the divided character of the poetry. As has become clear from a study of her poetic development, Plath expresses antithetical attitudes toward existence, alternately speaking for life and against it. At one moment the poems are expressions of power and vitality; in the next they are suicidal and self-negating. They embody what might be called a negative vitalism, brilliantly extolling and, simultaneously, harshly denying the claims of life. Plath both wants and does not want to live; both desires and does not desire to die. The poetry fixes itself in our minds through the sheer power of her language; yet we must —if we are to go on living—reject many of her attitudes and stances. If poetry is a mode of living, a method of making existence bearable, then Plath commits much of her energy to destroying what exists for herself and of rejecting the realities of the world for a more attractive universe of death. Surely Plath's openness to suffering and to the violently contradictory relations between life and death make one question the value of her work.

Paradoxically, though, Plath's poetry provides a positive basis for approaching aesthetic problems. Plath understood poetry as possessing a dual aspect. The poem both represents personal suffering as an immediate existential phenomenon and transforms this negative experience through the process of initiation. Beginning in 1959, these two goals determined her choice of aesthetic approach, of form, and of language. In terms of aesthetic attitude, she felt that the audience must be brought closer to the dual experience of suffering and transformation than it could be within traditional poetic contexts. The lyric-dramatic mode of her later work springs from this awareness of the relationship between reader and poem. She uses dramatic address in "Winter Trees"; dramatic monologue in "Lady Lazarus," "A Birthday Present," and many other poems; interior dialogue in "Fever 103°." Whereas *The Colossus* contains only a few dramatic monologues, dramatic methods in the late poems predominate. *Three Women*, for example, is a radio play.

In terms of formal developments, Plath had earlier viewed the form of the poem as a protective barrier that could keep personal realities outside the text, as is obvious in her apprentice and early poems (1950–59). The poems after *The Colossus* envision form as a way of shaping the conflicting personal forces of the self. She develops a triadic stanza that is indebted to the terza rima of Dante but that dispenses with regular rhymes and regular line lengths. Instead, this stanzaic form, with its short lines and off-rhymes, allows her to move from one image to the next and from one linguistic level to another with great rapidity and ease. She is thus able to shape each poem to the particular pressures exerted by different moments of experience—from the strident cries of the child for its mother, which are rendered in the end-stopped lines of "Morning Song," to the drowsiness of the death-wish, expressed in the enjambed, linked lines of "Poppies in July."

Finally, the language of the poems changes from her earlier period to reflect a more direct relationship between the poet's actual speech—and thus her personal reality—and the poem itself. The ease of such late poems as "Lady Lazarus" and "Daddy" is produced through the combination of colloquialisms with the Latinate language found in the earlier work. The total effect of these aesthetic, formal, and linguistic changes is to give a new immediacy to her work: the poems seem to come straight from an actually suffering human being.

There are two important rationales for Plath's approach to poetry, and they deserve extended treatment in order to understand the successes and limitations of her achievement. First, she believed that the poem must give expression to the poet's own anguish because suffering has become the central fact of historical and personal existence. In this respect, her motto could be represented by the passage from Franz Kafka's letters that Anne Sexton used as the epigraph to her book of poems *All My Pretty Ones* (1961): "The books we need are the kind that act upon us like a misfortune, that make us suffer like the death of someone we love more than ourselves, that make us feel as though we were on the verge of suicide, or lost in a forest remote from all human habitation—a book should serve as the ax for the frozen sea within us."[2] Like many modern and postmodern writers, Plath found the twentieth century to be an era of dehumanization and violence that requires of the poet an extraordinary openness to suffering. Only by forcing the reader to face his own suffering through the poem can the realities of our metaphysical, psychological, and social moment be experienced. The poet's life therefore becomes representative of the personal crisis in modern life, and his own experience of confusion and pain becomes exemplary.

Yet if the consciousness of suffering must be communicated to an audience that is already numbed to its own pain by the numerous accounts of modern history, new means must be found to awaken readers. Plath attempts to solve this problem by conveying the sense of a continuously unfolding present moment. She places her speakers in a fluctuating present, during which perceptual alterations and associative leaps govern the course of the poem from moment to moment. Abstraction has no place in her late work because discursive language presumes a world that can be controlled, labeled, and fixed through words. Plath wants, on the contrary, to convey the arbitrary, dark fate that hangs over us all. The randomness and violence of contemporary life is well reflected in such works as "Mary's Song," "Lady Lazarus," and "Daddy." The poems jump with hallucinatory rapidity from mind to world, from life to death, and back again. The reader follows the ongoing course of consciousness in its fearful instability and impermanence. The extremity of Plath's work mirrors the violent realities of our cultural moment.

Second, Plath's characteristic methods derive from the need to present an inner transformative process that can alleviate the tremendous suffering of the present. The repetitive sequence of images, the colloquial language, and the shorthand of a private symbolic language all allow her to bring the reader into the sphere of personal transformation. Within the context of her own struggle for survival, Plath's personae embody extravagant versions of our own desire for self-creation and self-alteration. The "I" in Plath's work is always on the way toward a new state of being; the poet's task is to externalize the self without mediation in the objects and processes of the outer world. In such poems as "Elm," for example, the mind merges with the object it contemplates, expressing all internal perceptions in the language of the external world of objects. The poet commits herself to a change in consciousness as well as in physical shape. Literary distance is therefore deliberately sacrificed for a white-hot personal presence in the poem as images and ideas reinforce the movement toward a new personal identity.

The divided responses to Plath's work can be attributed in large part to this aesthetic program that places so high a value on immediacy and on identification with the suffering speaker. Immediacy indicates that the material of the poem has been brought to its audience with very few conventional transformations. The speaker's voice in Plath's poetry seems to reflect not a series of poetic conventions or contexts but a number of lived moments of experience. Literary distance normally prevents painful subject matter from leaping out of an aesthetic context into the experience of the reader, but at certain moments in Plath's work the reader may feel uneasy with the immediacy of Plath's words, as in this passage from "Lady Lazarus":

> Dying
> Is an art, like everything else.
> I do it exceptionally well.
>
> I do it so it feels like hell.
> I do it so it feels real.

In the combination of boasting and matter-of-factness, of philosophical generalization and colloquial directness, this passage could be the speech of a woman who is ready to take her life. The reader may decide that the death-wish expressed in this poem is more than a wish, that the suicide is actually occurring or about to occur, especially since Plath did take her own life. With its absurd rhymes ("well" / "hell" / "real") and its colloquial simplicity, the passage has the immediacy and directness of actual speech. We can easily forget that it is, in fact, part of a dramatic monologue in which the persona plays out various fantasies of suicide before participating in a fantastic metamorphic change. Plath's poem breathes in the atmosphere of a heightened personal myth, yet it generates disturbing responses that are more appropriate to realistic accounts of suffering. The reader can legitimately wonder whether Plath is the speaker in her poem or whether she has created a fantasized self-dramatization.

Many readers who reject Plath's work as exhibitionistic and self-pitying have obviously taken the view that the poems are directly autobiographical. The situation, however, is more complex. Plath's use of personal material serves a crucial and legitimate function in her work as long as the invented drama, as in "Lady Lazarus," possesses a dramatic structure that is essentially independent of the events in the poet's life. The structure of Plath's successful poems permits the reader to understand what is occurring with only the slimmest reference, or with no reference at all, to the poet's biography. The rationale for Plath's use of personal material and violent imagery is that she can move into areas of feeling and suffering that have not been tapped in other poetry. As a result, she rejects the effect of impersonality that much modern poetry achieves. She wishes the reader to confront the situation of the speaker so that the immediate data of experience emerge with a terrifying vividness. In this regard the process of identification is indispensable.

Identification with a character or speaker occurs, of course, whenever we read literature, but it has a special importance in Plath's work. The "I" of the poems invites the reader both to witness and to identify with her as she undergoes extreme experiences. Because the self is alternately depressive and aggressive in Plath's work, the reader must identify with violently contrasting modes of experience. The task of following and comprehending the poems thus becomes one with the reader's process of placing himself within the consciousness of the "I." The hallucinatory images and the sudden interruptions in thought will otherwise remain incomprehensible. Identification is the precondition—as it is not for most poetry—of understanding Plath's work.

The narrowing of literary distance and the process of identification can be seen in a poem like "Ariel," where the vortex of images sucks the reader into identifying with a clearly self-destroying journey. On a literal level, few readers would willingly accept this ride into nothingness. But, through its precise rendering of sensation, the poem becomes a temptation: it draws us into its beautiful aural and visual universe against our will. As the pace of the horseride quickens, the intensity of the visual effects becomes greater. The identification of the speaker with the world outside becomes more extreme; Plath's metaphors suggest a large degree of fusion between disparate objects, as in the lines "I / foam to wheat, a glitter of seas." The ride across the fields suddenly turns into an ocean voyage. The body then fuses with the external world. As the speaker's merger with the sun is completed, so is the reader's merger with her: the process of identification within the poem generates a corresponding identification on the part of the reader. If the speaker will be destroyed in the cauldron of energy, the sun, so the reader will be destroyed in the cauldron of the poem. The poem entices us into a kind of death—the experience of abandoning our bodies and selves.

Of course, the reader will not immediately give himself over to the kind of experience that Plath's poetry offers. The primitivistic assumptions of her work assure that many modern readers will initially resist the situations in which her personae find themselves: a woman who speaks to an elm ("Elm"); a father who bites his daughter's heart in two ("Daddy"); a housewife who "talks" to a magical birthday present hidden behind veils ("A Birthday Present"). Only when the reader identifies with the speaker as an existent being do these poems come alive. The apparently absurd situations must be seen as having a deep truth: the alienated nature of the woman speaker lies in the contorted shape of the elm tree; the father has actually hurt the daughter psychically; the veiled birthday present possesses its own malevolent intentions as projected upon it by the speaker. We tend to resist these assumptions even though depth psychology has shown the omnipresent nature of projection and splitting. Plath's poems carry with them the mark of archetypes. She exposes a primitive universe that enters the modern kitchen and erupts within the family. And certainly her projections and fantasies are not so bizarre once we remember the primitive quality of mass political life during the twentieth century. Her treatment of fantasy and reality as interchangeable aspects of mental life places her closer to the actuality of contemporary existence than would any rationalistic assumption or theory.

Within the context of an aesthetics that emphasizes transformation and immediacy, Plath's choice of dramatic and quasi-dramatic forms in the late work can be explained. She wished to rid her poetry of the least trace of a literary or bookish quality that would come between the reader and the speaker's voice. To address someone else in a poem is to include the other as an actual presence within the poem. It is also to give a special urgency and directness to the poet's own voice, since the choice of an audience defines the specific location and character of the speaker. But in Plath's case particularly, the address to the other has violent consequences: the other is almost always a persecutor, who threatens the speaker's existence. By choosing to use dramatic address and dramatic monologues, Plath places her personae in direct contact with a figure who threatens them with death.

The power of the other over the speaker's existence makes a lyric-dramatic mode the natural choice for Plath's work. The figures and objects whom she addresses embody the life-and-death alternatives that consistently face her. It is thus not surprising to find that she capitalizes the names of the others to indicate their demonic nature. The most significant entities in her universe possess a supernatural power: The Other, who appears at her doorstep; the Nazi Doktor, who is more a demon than a fascist; Daddy, who plays numerous terrifying roles; and The Jailor, who imprisons a woman in a world of death. Although these characters are based upon real individuals, they assume their position in a fundamentally magical universe, where every encounter between self and other may produce terror or death. For a poet fascinated by the Tarot and by primitive rituals, the belief in such demonic figures is not surprising. She had begun early in her career to construct a private Greek mythology of colossi, oracles, and muses, and later she broadened it to include such figures as The Hanging Man (from the Tarot), the Other, and the Rival.

Plath's extreme fear of the other is accurately reflected in the dramatically heightened encounters that appear throughout the later poetry. In such poems as "The Bee Meeting," "A Birthday Present," and "The Other," the other person is not a specific individual but a powerful composite psychic symbol of the poet's relations to others. The other is projected outward from the poet's mind and then made part of a dramatic action. By building up a texture of symbolic references and notations that center upon this figure, the speaker can raise the personal conflict to a comprehensive symbolic level. In the archaic, divided world of Plath's poetry, the other must be cajoled, begged, and, ultimately, overcome if the self is to survive. The ultimate object of these dramas remains survival through self-transformation.

Yet the self does not, finally, survive, and this failure of the transformative process casts a negative light on even those poems in which Plath does enact a positive movement toward self-transcendence. Since criticism comes after the fact of creation and, in Plath's case, after the suicide, critics have a tendency to view all of a poet's work in the light of a single idea or a single poem: they see Plath as a poet of suicide. But the reality is that her poems embody both her faith in the transforming powers of art and initiatory process and her despair of altering her psychological condition and her relation to others. The contradictory emotions of her poetry provide great dynamic power at the same time as they undermine any consistency of intellectual or philosophical attitude. The work gathers its force from a seething conflict within the poet, but Plath sacrifices coherence to the overwhelming intensity of the conflict. The psychology of the poet interferes with her expression of both order and energy.

The psychological dimensions of Plath's situation have been often discussed, although such discussions typically throw little light on the question of her achievement as a poet.[3] The importance of psychological understanding in Plath's case actually resides in the psychological aspects of her aesthetic program. From this point of view we can see the meaning of the initiatory process for her and the consequences of her failure to extend its death-and-rebirth pattern successfully into all aspects of her existence. The divisions that Plath's readers have experienced within her work then appear as the results of the fatal psychological divisions within her sense of self.

Psychologically, the aesthetics of transformation and immediacy can be understood as a means of reuniting the self and the world through poetry. In general, Plath sees the world either as an inert, unresponsive hardness, symbolized by stone, or as a dangerous otherness, symbolized by devouring others. The first mode of union characterizes *The Colossus*, with its statue, pebbles, and rocks, particularly in such poems as "The Colossus," "The Disquieting Muses," "Hermit at Outermost House," and "Point Shirley." The second mode dominates in *Ariel* and *Winter Trees*, with their images of mouths, gaping holes, and abysses, and with the prevalence of violent deaths and wounds from knives in poems like "Daddy," "Cut," and "A Birthday Present." With the ego separated in these two ways from the external object, life appears as either senseless (blank, bald, hard) or terrifying (voracious, cannibalistic).

If the separated ego and the outside world can fuse in a controlled way, however, then life can possess the vitality that it had before birth and during early childhood. The poem becomes the method by which the lost personal being of the world is recaptured. When Plath attempts to regain the "blood-hot" and "personal" reality of the earlier world, she turns back inevitably to the images and symbols of her childhood world: water, dead father, mother, bees, and the sea. In this respect her career possesses an admirable unity. She dramatizes in the later work a universe of magical potentialities and animistic phenomena because the child world was magical. By forcing the world to repeat itself, she hopes to bring reality back to the shape and vitality it once had.

The major consequence of this desire is Plath's wish to alter the shape of her body. Since the adult body stands between the self and the world, she wants to negate her identification with the vulnerable and hated body. This is one of the reasons why poems like "Lady Lazarus" and "Fever 103°" enact a process of abandoning the body. Only by remaking the body in a new form, which is imagined in the poem, can Plath find the freedom she had experienced as a child. The body may be replaced and revitalized, as in "The Stones"; or burned down, as in "Lady Lazarus"; or vaporized, as in "The Detective"; or magically transformed, as in "Fever 103°." There are many methods, but the goal remains the same: union of the body with the objects that surround it.

Plath's psychological project is therefore both self-negating and self-expansive. She wants to destroy identity and then enlarge the scope of the self until it encompasses the entire world. But this desire to make the body and the world one implicates her in a series of destructive processes and maneuvers over which she loses control. Given the extremity of her rejection of the body, her failure to achieve unity seems almost inevitable. We all at various moments wish to flee from our bodies because they make us vulnerable to attack and pain, but we also strive to protect the body from threatening external forces. We avoid identification with the body because it moves us toward death at the same time that we identify with it in order to prolong our physical existence. This ambivalent attitude appears to be a permanent aspect of our being in the world: to give up all connection to our bodies would be to cease existing, at least as existence is normally understood. Plath's intention of reshaping the body therefore involves her in a trap. If she abandons her body to free the self, she plunges toward her death; but if she props up the ego in its battle with the body, she remains in a state of living death.

Caught in this losing situation, Plath most frequently plays out the consequences of divorcing herself from the body. In "Cut," for example, she addresses her own thumb in hysterical shock; in "The Courage of Shutting Up," she speaks of her own brain as a record that can play back all the "accounts of bastardies" in her life. In the more violent forms of this separa-

tion from the body, Plath imagines death by fire or mutilation
or murder. Or, in a more meditative mood, she fantasizes the
peaceful passing away of the body as the self watches, as in
"Tulips" and "Last Words." Whatever the method of dying,
she confronts a structural obstacle to any attempt at overcom-
ing the dualism of self and world: the self will not become
spontaneous and vital because it is frozen in its fear of death.
And to lose the death-fear by plunging into death is, of course,
to lose all vitality.

The only possible resolution to the trap Plath faces is the
initiatory process. Initiation solves the dilemma of the self by
deliberately engaging death in a symbolic battle. Since the self
must die before it can become free, the initiatory ritual simu-
lates the death of the initiate and his merger with the world. In
the incorporative strategy of the ritual, the man or woman
returns symbolically to the mother's womb and to the womb
of the earth, thus recapitulating his or her origins. To be
incorporated into the earth and the mother once again is to die,
but it is also to gain a second chance at life. Freed from a
compulsive grasping onto life, the initiate comes back from
isolation, symbolic mutilation, or circumcision as one of those
who has died and been reborn, that is, as a metaphysically
altered individual. The body that has been cut or symbolically
torn apart is reintegrated and can no longer be identified with
the body that has previously sinned or experienced fear and
guilt. The body emerges fresh and whole, with the innocent
reality of the newborn. As in Plath's celebration of her children
or in her metaphoric transformations into a new shape, the
baby is the model of the initiatory recreation of the self, for the
baby lives unbounded by conceptions of time or space or by
anxieties over right or wrong.

It is not accidental that Plath in the late 1950s was attracted
to African and archaic modes of understanding the universe.
Her relationship to self and world constituted a sealed prison
unless she could break out of the walls of the isolated ego. The
"primitive" stories that she found in Paul Radin's *African Folk-*

tales and Sculpture confirmed that her personal material was, in fact, universal fantasy and that transformative processes could be harnessed to free the self. The death-and-rebirth pattern of initiation reflected her own sense of having been reborn after her suicide attempt and mental breakdown in 1953, and she used this pattern in her account of that period in *The Bell Jar*. Personal psychology and the reading of archaic materials converged to make initiation the central obsession of her poetry after 1959, but even before then she had known that initiation was a crucial subject for her. In the short story "Initiation" (1953), her main character, a girl undergoing a sorority hazing, states that her initiation into the world had just begun.[4]

The initiatory character of Plath's last poems provides them with both energy and accuracy. Plath found in initiation a precise language for her obsessive imaginings of death. Plath's uniqueness clearly appears in lines like these from "Elm":

> I have suffered the atrocity of sunsets.
> Scorched to the root
> My red filaments burn and stand, a hand of wires.
>
> Now I break up in pieces that fly about like clubs.
> A wind of such violence
> Will tolerate no bystanding: I must shriek.
>
> [*A*, p. 15]

The speaker is the elm tree, which means that the metaphoric comparison of branches to a "hand" occurs from the other side of natural being. The tree uses a human metaphor just as the human speaker will use a natural metaphor at the end of the poem in speaking of her own body: "What is this, this face / So murderous in its tangle of branches?—" (*A*, p. 16). The face is both the speaker's own violent nature projected onto the tree and the tree's own natural "face." Nature looks at us as we look at nature. The equivalence between tree and woman asserts a crucial identity among all living things in the universe. Plath demonstrates here, as elsewhere in her poems, the ability to externalize her self and body in objects and to think through these objects.

We have been repeatedly told by modernist critics that thinking concretely is the sine qua non of the modern poet; but Plath goes further than almost any recent poet in converting the physical and animate elements of the world into a language. Plath uses landscape, for instance, to formulate her own set of symbolic objects. The most remarkable aspect of such poems as "The Moon and the Yew Tree" is that she extensively and persuasively adopts objects as specific symbols for personal experience—the moon is a negative mother image; the yew tree, her dead father. In "Sheep in Fog" the sheep become symbols of the quick passage of love. A passage from Octavio Paz's essay on archaic poetries suggests the orientation of Plath's symbolic language: "The rigor of the 'logic of the senses' of primitive peoples amazes us by its intellectual precision, but the richness of their perceptions is no less extraordinary: where a modern nose distinguishes only a vague odor, a savage perceives a precise range of different smells. What is most astonishing is the method, the manner of associating all these signs [of the physical world], so that in the end they are woven into a series of symbolic objects: the world converted into a physical language."[5] Surely it is Plath's method of associating and the precision of her associations that is most marvelous about her poems. Her poetry possesses a "physical language" that goes hand in hand with her initiatory project: the desire to reincorporate herself into the world's body. What Paz finds most remarkable in archaic poetry gives Plath's work its uniqueness and power. Her poems register relationships and distinctions in the natural world that most of us pass by without noticing. They are attuned to the archaic world and its insistence on thinking through objects and sensations rather than through abstractions and conceptions.

Yet Plath's imaginative affinity with archaic modes of thought also points to the great irony of her work. The beauty of her images, the precision of her associations, and the bril-

liance of her formal invention testify not to life's order, but to
death's harsh grip on the world. In her own fury or depression,
she hammers out a language that pushes poetry ever closer to
the objects it contemplates. Her linguistic goal is to summon a
reality that will supplant the world of death, but the eventual
result contradicts her aim. The fear of death produces a shrill-
ness in her life that leads her to greater depression and then to
greater efforts at self-negation. Negation spreads from the self
outward to the other and ultimately to the entire cosmos. Even
though the poem envisions magnificent fusions between the
threatened body and the external world, it finds no consis-
tent, continuous principle of organization that will prevail over
death. Although ritual time is eternal—pure duration without
interruption—the self cannot long exist within this state of
being. The self shatters its own reality but cannot, finally,
discover a comprehensive field of being into which it fits.

Inevitably, Plath's work does not express what the poet
herself would have wished to express. The vitalistic, positive
current of her poetry runs exactly counter to its hysterical,
self-annihilating force. No poet in recent memory has so ex-
plicitly embraced the opposite extremes of existence at once.
At one moment Plath's poems express the most intimate con-
tact with nature, as in this description of poppies in "Poppies
in October":

> A gift, a love gift
> Utterly unasked for
> By a sky
>
> Palely and flamily
> Igniting its carbon monoxides, by eyes
> Dulled to a halt under bowlers.
>
> [*A*, p. 19]

The magnificence of the poppies survives beneath the deathly
sky, with its poisons, and amid the enervated men under their
bowlers. Beauty emerges in the midst of a killing nature. But

in another poem, the saving brilliance of flower or animal has totally evaporated, and the poet remains with her own self-obsession: "The nights snapped out of sight like a lizard's eyelid: / A world of bald white days in a shadeless socket" ["The Hanging Man," *A*, p. 69]. Visionary brilliance gives way to visionary deadness.

Still, Plath provides the most precise visions of suffering and death found in American poetry in the 1960s. She brings an intensity to her presentation of pain that elevates the subject matter beyond autobiographical realities, as in this passage from "Fever 103°":

> The tongues of hell
> Are dull, dull as the triple
>
> Tongues of dull, fat Cerberus
> Who wheezes at the gate. Incapable
> Of licking clean
>
> The aguey tendon, the sin, the sin.
> The tinder cries.
> The indelible smell
>
> Of a snuffed candle.
>
> [*A*, p. 53]

The associative processes here are as quick as those in any recent poetry, and they suggest a tremendous vitality. The tendons of the body, aching from the "ague," are the physical equivalent of the sinning mind, aching from guilt and self-punishment. The crying of the "tinder" is, of course, the "tender" cry of the body; the smell of the snuffed candle is indelible in the physical world because the speaker's suffering is unforgettable in her inner world. In nine short lines Plath has compressed a vision of hell that works back and forth between mind and body, including allusions both to Greek and Christian notions of suffering. In its daring metaphoric jumps, the passage exemplifies Plath's ability to take us into the heart of the endless struggle between consciousness and physical reality.

Although other contemporary American poets have vividly described the relations between suffering and the individual self, Plath's initiatory approach and her related methods separate her from such contemporaries as Robert Lowell, John Berryman, and Anne Sexton. Certainly all these poets responded to a powerful shared cultural and psychological situation. Each was dissatisfied with the social and academic consensus of the 1950s. For several reasons, American poetry in this period turned away from its formalist moorings and looked to Beat, surrealist, and Romantic influences: the ending of the Cold War mentality of the Eisenhower years; the pressure of constantly living under the threat of nuclear annihilation; personal dissatisfaction with the increasing regimentation and conformity in American life. These trends influenced poets toward a reevaluation of their aesthetic practice. The similarity in the psychological and family histories of Lowell, Berryman, Sexton, and Plath suggests another reason for the convergence of their interests on personal suffering. Robert Lowell had been in and out of mental hospitals for years; John Berryman's alcoholism grew steadily worse; Anne Sexton had also been a mental patient and was suicidal; Plath had attempted suicide. But these general cultural and biographical factors provided only the framework of concerns within which these writers worked. Plath is marked by the method she chose in transforming the personality through poetry: her commitment to the initiatory process, the use of image sequences, and a lyric-dramatic mode.

John Berryman and Robert Lowell are poets of an entirely different type. Although Plath learned from both of them, she did not imitate them in her final period. Like Berryman, she was obsessed with suicide: both poets' fathers died when they were young, Berryman's from self-inflicted wounds. Both concern themselves, in different ways, with grief and loss. But Berryman's *The Dream Songs*, his central poem, uses a

single persona throughout. Berryman employs Henry to tie
together a series of basically discrete monologues about loss
and grief. The interweaving of literary references, personal
reminiscences, and political commentary in a highly stylized
but broken-down "blackface" English makes *The Dream Songs* a
panorama of Berryman's, and the country's, psychic and cul-
tural dislocations. The fact that Plath herself is mentioned in
several songs and made the subject of song 172 suggests how
different Berryman's form is from Plath's: Plath wrote no
poems about other poets or about topical issues. Furthermore,
she wrote no long poems; only "Daddy" approaches the lin-
guistic disjointedness that Berryman aims for:

> I'm scared a lonely.
> Never see my son,
> easy not to see anyone,
> combers out to sea
> know they're goin somewhere but not me.
> Got a little poison, got a little gun,
> I'm scared a lonely.[6]

This first part of song 40 is at the opposite end of the spec-
trum, emotionally and linguistically, from Plath's poetry, even
though it deals with suicide.

Even more than Berryman, Lowell found it necessary to
develop the strategies of the persona to represent the course
of American cultural life. The various versions of *Notebooks
1967–68* play on a Robert Lowell who is alternately a pub-
lic personality and a private man with sorrows and difficul-
ties. The intertwining of public and private selves in Lowell's
work provides a framework for sometimes brilliant, sometimes
trivial revelations. Unlike Plath, Lowell never attempts the
kind of poem that totally drops the mediation of personality
through history or social role. Even *Life Studies*, which has
been hailed as a confessional work, carefully manipulates a
representative figure through a variety of historical periods:
childhood in the 1920s; political imprisonment in the forties;

marriage and psychological disturbance in the forties and fifties. The periodization of *Life Studies*, as well as its careful autobiographical analyses, marks it as a diametrically different type of work from *Ariel* or *Winter Trees*. Lowell's orientation is toward analysis, Plath's toward myth. Whereas Lowell tends toward the refinement of personality, Plath wishes to abolish the self altogether. Of the writers of personal poetry during the late fifties and early sixties, Plath and Lowell are the opposites who define the shape of a period's obsession: the disintegration of the individual self and the search for meaning and value in a new kind of poetry.

Anne Sexton's work, on the other hand, defines how extraordinary a poet Plath really is. Working with similar material, particularly the subjects of suicide and madness, Sexton produces poems of sociological and biographical interest. The immediacy of Plath's work is absent in Sexton's because the tension between speaker and reader has collapsed. Sexton's poetry suggests no more than nonstop diary reading: the audience does not exist as a force inside or outside the poem. The poems suggest that they will enter into the complexities of the self, but they turn into loose-jointed, self-indulgent monologues. Encountering nothing outside them of significance, they tend to be wordy, repetitious, and self-inflated. These faults could be exemplified at length from any of Sexton's volumes, but a good contrast with Plath lies in the comparison of "Daddy" with this passage from "Those Times . . . ," a childhood reminiscence in Sexton's *Live or Die* (1966):

> I will speak of the childhood cruelties,
> being a third child,
> the last given
> and the last taken—
> of the nightly humiliations when Mother undressed me,
> of the life of the daytime, locked in my room—
> being the unwanted, the mistake
> that Mother used to keep Father
> from his divorce.

> Divorce!
> The romantic's friend,
> romantics who fly into maps
> of other countries,
> hips and noses and mountains,
> into Asia or the Black Forest,
> or caught by 1928,
> the year of the *me*,
> by mistake,
> not for divorce
> but instead.[7]

The problem with Sexton's poem lies, first, in its failure to objectify the memories of Father and Mother. While Plath leaves no possibility for doubt about the nature of Daddy, dramatizing each moment of awareness or memory of him, Sexton begins portentously—"I will speak of the childhood cruelties, . . ."—and then provides only vague references to what happened to her as a child. The "humiliations" when she undressed are unspecified, for example, although it is not clear why she felt humiliated in front of her mother. No clear image emerges of her father or mother, whereas "Daddy" brilliantly enlarges the memory of Plath's father to legendary proportions. Plath dramatizes the situation between daughter and father as if no time had passed since the father's death: the emotional situation is still burning in her consciousness. But Sexton's words suggest someone who is trying to call up a strong emotion that has lost much of its original power.

Second, Sexton's poem is marred by the triviality of its associations. It jumps from personal reference to personal reference, never elevating the material to anything more than personal nostalgia and grief. If 1928 is the "year of the *me*," according to the poem, then the reader has the right to know why this *me* is of significance. The poet assumes a self-importance that she does not demonstrate; she becomes involved in her autobiography. But Plath is not interested in detailing the facts of her life—the year of her birth, the marital difficulties of her parents, the nature of the parents' argument over divorce—but in presenting the processes of consciousness. "Daddy" is brilliant because of its wide-ranging associations to Nazism, to Freudian theories, and to ritual patterns. The wildness of the emotion is contained and channeled through these structures, whereas Sexton's work exemplifies the worst aspects of confessionalism: an impulse to confess without adequate means to transform the personal material.

Viewed from the perspective of her initiatory project, then, Plath appears as a unique and disturbing figure in American poetry. She is a poet of enormous talent, who pushes toward a vitalistic account of human existence in its relation to a hostile external reality. Yet she fails to believe in her own theoretical and positive program sufficiently to overcome the corrosive effects of death-fear and death-longing. She enacts repeatedly a drama that can terminate in either life or death, using poetry as a means of playing out the alternate fates reserved for her by existence. The discrete moments of unity and ecstasy in her work anticipate a greater unity of thought and sensation, but that unification of diversity never emerges. As she returns again and again to the same symbolically charged landscapes and the same figures of death and suffering, she seems to lose faith in the ultimate triumph of the life force over the forces of negation. The process of self-transformation winds down into self-annihilation.

Yet it is perhaps absurd to expect that Plath by herself could present an integrated vision of body and mind, of life and death. Our culture has been riddled since Puritan times with intense divisions within its system of ideals and its versions of human purpose. Plath reflects a gigantic split within American culture between its positive valuation of a fierce selfhood and its radical denial of the body's sufficiency. Plath is unusual in the extremity of her rejection of the body, but her search for self-expansion through a denial of the surrounding physical reality—of the body, of the social system, of the limitations of time and space—is the essential American story. The representative figure of the American quest for self-transcendence is Melville's Ahab, who sails out to revenge his mutilated body in defiance of the physical and metaphysical restraints on the self. His inevitable death can stand for the death of many American literary seekers, F. Scott Fitzgerald's Gatsby, William Faulkner's Quentin Compson, Nathanael West's Miss Lonelyhearts, not to speak of the numerous writers themselves who have ended their search in despair or suicide.

American literature records the unnatural death of its protagonists so often that Plath's poems should shock us less than they do. But, as Leslie Fiedler pointed out years ago in his *Love and Death in the American Novel*, Americans have a tremendous ability to ignore the negative force of their masterpieces and to read them as a species of children's fairytales. In Plath's work, of course, this response is impossible. While an optimistic American public can turn to Robert Frost as a benign nature poet and to Herman Melville as a writer of hearty sea adventures, Plath resists this desire for a happy ending, as do her poems. Her work is as physical a manifestation as language can give of the tremendous yet vicious energies latent in American life. When she speaks of killing her composite father-husband or of destroying her own body, she is personalizing the plot that runs throughout American literature, most evidently in our fiction: Melville's whale-killing; Faulkner's epic of generational torment; Hemingway's ritual encounters with death. Or when she dramatizes the antithetical situation of victimization, of being tortured by others, the poetry opens up the suffering that is almost always present beneath the surface of our best authors: Emily Dickinson's unbearable sensitivity to others; Robert Frost's fear of darkness and nothingness; T. S. Eliot's isolation and alienation. The great difference in Plath is that she plays out this essential American story on the field of her own body. The best of her poems seem to tear her body apart in the quest for transformation. Still, this process is simply an internalized version of the journey Melville describes in *Moby*

Dick: the attempt to reduce the irrational otherness of the whale, and thus existence itself, to the will of the self.

Finally, Plath's quest for initiatory change fails because the other cannot be brought under the domination of the self, even when the self wills its own destruction so as to merge with the world. Her fierce and brilliant language is all directed at the other whom she wishes to overcome, but the giants and colossi of her poetry fall down only to rise again; the body immolates itself only to return to its old, guilt-ridden shape. As Kafka says, the suffering the artist undergoes releases him—for more suffering. Plath's initiatory dramas release her from one state of suffering so that she may endure a new agony. For the briefest moment, though, she is set free from the imprisonment of selfhood; and it is this moment that her best poems, "Ariel," "Fever 103°," "Lady Lazarus," and "The Couriers," celebrate. If she could not sustain her liberation beyond the moment, she still provides an intense vision of the irreducible, entwined core of life and death.

Notes

Chapter 1

1. John Berryman, *The Dream Songs*, p. 191.
2. Anne Sexton, "Sylvia's Death," in "The Barfly Ought to Sing," p. 179.
3. Robert Lowell, Foreword to *Ariel*, p. ix. All further references to Sylvia Plath's poetry and prose will be identified within the body of the text by the following abbreviations: *Ariel (A)*; *The Colossus (C)*; *Crossing the Water (CW)*; *Lyonnesse (L)*; *Crystal Gazer (CG)*; *Pursuit (P)*.
4. Stephen Spender, "Warnings from the Grave," p. 202.
5. For Greer's comment, see Harriet Rosenstein, "Reconsidering Sylvia Plath," p. 12.
6. Phyllis Chesler, *Women and Madness*, p. 12.
7. Robin Morgan, *Monster*, p. 78.
8. Sylvia Plath, "Context," pp. 45–46.
9. A. Alvarez, *The Savage God*, p. 251. Italics added.
10. Plath, "Context," p. 46.
11. Sylvia Plath, BBC Interview with Peter Orr, in *The Poet Speaks*, pp. 167–68.
12. For the psychoanalytic accounts of Plath's suicide, see Edward Butscher, *Sylvia Plath*, and James Hoyle, "Sylvia Plath," pp. 187–203. The explanation for the suicide as a "cry for help" is offered by Nancy Hunter Steiner, *A Closer Look at Ariel*, pp. 82–83.
13. M. L. Rosenthal, "Sylvia Plath," pp. 83, 86–87.
14. Butscher, *Plath*, p. xi.
15. Plath, BBC Interview, pp. 167–68.
16. Robert Lowell, *Life Studies*, p. 76.
17. Marjorie Perloff, *The Poetic Art of Robert Lowell*, p. 86.
18. Lowell, *Life Studies*, p. 62.

Chapter 2

1. Sylvia Plath, "Initiation," p. 94.
2. Sylvia Plath, "Ocean 1212-W," p. 266.
3. See, particularly, Mircea Eliade, *Rites and Symbols of Initiation* and *Myth and Reality*.
4. Eliade, *Rites and Symbols*, p. xiv.
5. Elizabeth Hardwick, for example, takes Plath's suicide as the key to her poetry. See *Seduction and Betrayal*, especially pp. 114–229.
6. See, for example, Joseph Campbell, *The Hero with a Thousand Faces*, pp. 28–30; and Eliade, *Rites and Symbols*, p. 130.

7. Sylvia Plath, "The Jailor," p. 51.

8. According to Ted Hughes's account, in "Notes on the Chronological Order of Sylvia Plath's Poems," p. 192.

9. Theodore Roethke, *Collected Poems*, p. 74.

10. Paul Radin, *African Folktales and African Sculpture*.

11. Ibid., p. 250.

12. Eliade, *Rites and Symbols*, especially pp. 51–60.

13. See Irving Howe, "Sylvia Plath," p. 92.

Chapter 3

1. Almost all of what I call the "apprentice poetry" has been published in the two limited-edition collections, *Crystal Gazer* and *Lyonnesse*. Poems that have been published only in magazines await a collected edition of Plath's poetry, which is planned by Harper & Row, New York.

2. The list of American poets who shifted away from the traditional forms in the 1958–63 period is impressive. Aside from Plath, Lowell, and Wright, there were W. S. Merwin, Philip Levine, and James Dickey. In the fifties, Allen Ginsberg, Robert Duncan, Robert Creeley, and the San Francisco poets campaigned vigorously for free-form experimentation. Charles Olson championed William Carlos Williams's antitraditional position and introduced the concept of free-field composition. Surrealist and contemporary French influences came to American attention via John Ashberry and the work of Robert Bly's *The Fifties* magazine. Bly was instrumental in waging critical warfare against the southern traditional influences of John Crowe Ransom and Allen Tate and in translating, with Wright, Latin-American surrealists like Pablo Neruda and César Vallejo and German neoromantics like Rainer Maria Rilke and Georg Trakl. All these critical and poetic pressures came to bear upon academic poets toward the end of the 1950s, encouraging movement toward the colloquial and the free form. The critical resistance to these changes was at first strong, as the division between academic and Beat poetries and anthologies would indicate. But when well-known poets like Theodore Roethke and Lowell moved away from Anglo-American modernist influences, which were essentially traditional, the resistance became less intense. No full-length account of American poetry in the 1950s and 1960s exists, though there are helpful chapters on different poets in M. L. Rosenthal's *The New Poets*.

3. Philip Levine, "Looking for an Opening," pp. 388–92. The quotations in the paragraph are taken from pages 388, 391, and 390.

4. As reported by Ted Hughes, in "Notes on the Chronological Order of Sylvia Plath's Poems," p. 188.

5. Sylvia Plath, "Second Winter," pp. 10–11.

6. John Crowe Ransom, "Eclogue," *Selected Poems*, p. 13.

7. John Crowe Ransom, "Prometheus in Straits," ibid., p. 59.

8. Sylvia Plath, "Dialogue en Route," pp. 239–40.

9. Dylan Thomas, "I See the Boys of Summer," *The Collected Poems of Dylan Thomas*, p. 3.

10. Thomas, "The Force that through the Green Fuse Drives the Flower," ibid., p. 10.

11. Wallace Stevens, "Man and Bottle," *The Collected Poems of Wallace Stevens*, p. 238.

12. Sylvia Plath, "Doomsday," p. 29.

13. Sylvia Plath, "To Eva Descending the Stair," p. 63.

14. Sylvia Plath, "Temper of Time," p. 119.

15. Ibid.

16. Sylvia Plath, "Dream with Clamdiggers," pp. 232–33.

17. Sylvia Plath, "Two Lovers and a Beachcomber by the Real Sea," pp. 52, 54.

18. See, for example, reviews by Bernard Bergonzi, "The Ransom Note," p. 9, and Dom Moraes, review of *The Colossus*, p. 1413.

19. I am indebted for this observation to Jerome Francis Megna, "The Two-World Division in the Poetry of Sylvia Plath," p. 34.

20. Sylvia Plath, "Letter to a Purist," p. 855.

21. "After the Funeral," *The Collected Poems of Dylan Thomas*, p. 96.

22. Reading Jacques Cousteau's account of his diving expeditions triggered both this poem and "Full Fathom Five," according to Ted Hughes, in "Notes," pp. 189–90.

23. The poems included in the so-called Cambridge MS have been printed in "The Cambridge Collection," pp. 248–53. Stanzas 4 and 5, which bear upon the following discussion, are:

> A man who used to clench
> Bees in his fist
> And out-ran the thundercrack,
> That one: not known enough: death's trench
> Digs him into my quick:
> At each move I confront his ready ghost
>
> Glaring sunflower-eyed
> From the glade of hives,
> Antlered by bramble-hat,
> Berry-juice purpling his thumbs: o I'd
> Run time aground before I met
> His match. Luck's hard which falls to love
>
> Such long gone darlings. . . .

24. The reason given by Ingrid Melander in *The Poetry of Sylvia Plath*, p. 36, is surely not correct. Melander claims that Plath was embarrassed by the personal tone used in relation to the father in stanzas 4 and 5. Yet the tone of "The Beekeeper's Daughter," which does appear in *The Colossus*, is virtually identical to that of the omitted stanzas in "All the Dead Dears."

25. The title is taken from a painting by Giorgio de Chirico, "I Musi Inquietanti." Details of the muses themselves—bald, stitched heads, and blank faces—seem to come from this and other de Chirico paintings, although baldness and blankness are qualities ascribed by Plath to a number of feared objects.

26. See Sylvia Plath, *The Bell Jar*, p. 69: "I started out by dressing in a white coat and sitting on a white stool in a room with four cadavers, while Buddy and his friends cut them up. These cadavers were so unhuman-looking they didn't bother me a bit. They had stiff, leathery, purple-black skin and they smelt like old pickle jars."

27. This line is also, as M. L. Rosenthal points out, a grotesque parody of "The Love Song of J. Alfred Prufrock": "In the room the women come and go" ("Metamorphoses of a Book," p. 456).

28. Piero Bianconi, *The Complete Paintings of Breughel*, p. 95.

Chapter 4

1. See Ted Hughes, "Sylvia Plath's *Crossing the Water*," pp. 165–72.

2. Hughes indicates that some selections had been made for *Ariel*, but it is not clear from his account exactly which poems Plath had wanted or how far along in the selection process she was ("Notes on the Chronological Order of Sylvia Plath's Poems," p. 193).

3. "The first poem of the final phase," writes Hughes, "was ELM" (Ibid., p. 193). "Elm" was written in April 1962.

4. The exceptions are "Insomniac," which won first prize at the Cheltenham Poetry Festival in the summer of 1961 and was published in the Festival program, and "Stillborn" and "Last Words," which were published post-humously. The ten poems reprinted from the British edition of *The Colossus* in *Crossing the Water* date, of course, from before 1960. The note at the beginning of *Crossing the Water* correctly names the ten poems, but incorrectly states: "*Nine* of the poems here were published in the British edition of *The Colossus*."

5. The figure is approximate, since unpublished work may appear in *The Collected Poems* that is planned by Harper & Row.

6. Sylvia Plath, "The Jailor," p. 51.

7. The fourth and fifth lines of the poem are probably addressed to the lost child: "Your absence is inconspicuous; / Nobody can tell what I lack." This observation derives from Eileen Aird, *Sylvia Plath*, p. 53.

8. Sylvia Plath, "Stars over the Dordogne," pp. 346–47.

Chapter 5

1. Barbara Hardy calls "The Couriers" that "most baffling poem" in "The Poetry of Sylvia Plath," p. 181. Jerome Megna denies its internal coherence: "The poem itself, having little internal logic, rather reflects the speaker's depressed state of mind" ("The Two-World Division in The Poetry of Sylvia Plath," p. 158).

2. Sylvia Plath, "The Jailor," p. 51.

3. During the transitional period, Plath wrote two poems addressed to her daughter Frieda, "Magi" and "You're," and one that alludes briefly to her, "Candles." The late work includes nine poems on children. Seven are about her son Nick, "Morning Song," Brasília," "The Night Dances," "Nick and the Candlestick," "Child," "By Candlelight," and "For a Fatherless Son"; one is about Nick and Frieda, "Balloons"; and the remaining poem deals with a thalidomide baby, "Thalidomide."

4. Sylvia Plath, "On the Decline of Oracles," pp. 368–69.

5. The epigraph was quoted from a manuscript of a book on de Chirico that Plath had read by James Thrall Soby, *Giorgio de Chirico*, p. 248. Cf. Ingrid Melander, *The Poetry of Sylvia Plath*, p. 37. One detail in the poem, the god's white head above a curtain, seems to have been taken from the de Chirico painting "L'Enigme de l'Oracle."

6. Sylvia Plath, "November Graveyard," p. 134.

7. Sylvia Plath "Electra on Azalea Path," p. 415.

8. One earlier reference to the father as black man, "Man in Black" (*C*, pp. 52–3), does not connect him, as the *Ariel* poems do, with oppression.

9. Quoted by A. Alvarez in "Sylvia Plath," p. 65. The note to "Daddy" was originally to be read along with the poem on a BBC program that was never actually broadcast.

10. A. Alvarez reports Plath's words in "Sylvia Plath," p. 66: "When she first read me the poem a few days after she wrote it, she called it a piece of 'light verse.'"

11. For the autobiographical background to "The Other" and "Lesbos," see Butscher, *Sylvia Plath*, pp. 322–24, 333.

12. A. Alvarez, *The Savage God*, p. 31.

Chapter 6

1. Franz Kafka, in conversation with G. Janouch, as quoted by Dore Ashton, *Philip Guston*, p. 9.

2. Anne Sexton, *All My Pretty Ones*, n.p.

3. See, for example, the jargon-ridden psychoanalytic treatment by David Holbrook in *Sylvia Plath*, in which the poems become nothing more than a code for a psychotic's suicidal drive. This method not only casts no light on the poems; in Holbrook's hands, psychoanalysis descends to self-parody.

4. Sylvia Plath, "Initiation," p. 94.

5. Octavio Paz, *Conjunctions and Disjunctions*, p. 10.

6. John Berryman, *The Dream Songs*, p. 44.

7. Anne Sexton, *Live or Die*, p. 29.

Bibliography

Aird, Eileen. *Sylvia Plath*. New York: Barnes and Noble, 1974.

―――. "Variants in a Tape Recording of Fifteen Poems by Sylvia Plath." *Notes & Queries* 19 (February 1972): 59–61.

Alvarez, A. *The Savage God: A Study of Suicide*. New York: Random House, 1972.

―――. "Sylvia Plath." In *The Art of Sylvia Plath*, edited by Charles Newman, pp. 56–68. Bloomington: Indiana University Press, 1971.

―――. "Sylvia Plath: The Cambridge Collection." *Cambridge Review* 90, no. 2187 (7 February 1969): 246–53.

Ames, Lois. "Notes toward a Biography." *The Art of Sylvia Plath*, edited by Charles Newman, pp. 155–73. Bloomington: Indiana University Press, 1971.

Ashton, Dore. *Philip Guston*. New York: Grove Press, 1961.

Bagg, Robert. "The Rise of Lady Lazarus." *Mosaic* 2, no. 4 (Summer 1969): 9–36.

Bergonzi, Bernard. "The Ransom Note." *Manchester Guardian* no. 35,583 (25 November 1960), 9.

Berryman, John. *The Dream Songs*. New York: Farrar, Straus & Giroux, 1969.

Bianconi, Piero. *The Complete Paintings of Breughel*. New York: Harry N. Abrams, 1967.

Boyers, Robert. "Sylvia Plath: The Trepanned Veteran." *Centennial Review* 13, no. 2 (Spring 1969): 138–53.

Butscher, Edward. *Sylvia Plath: Method and Madness*. New York: Seabury Press, 1976.

C., M. W. "Remembering Sylvia." *Cambridge Review* 90, no. 2187 (7 February 1969): 253–54.

Campbell, Joseph. *The Hero with a Thousand Faces*. Princeton: Princeton University Press, 1949.

Chesler, Phyllis. *Women and Madness*. New York: Avon, 1972.

Claire, William F. "That Rare, Random Descent: The Poetry and

Paths of Sylvia Plath." *Antioch Review* 26 (Winter 1966–67): 552–60.

Cleverdon, Douglas. "On *Three Women.*" In *The Art of Sylvia Plath*, edited by Charles Newman, pp. 227–29. Bloomington: Indiana University Press, 1971.

Davison, Peter. "Inhabited by a Cry: The Last Poetry of Sylvia Plath." *Atlantic* 218 (August 1966): 76–77.

Dyson, A. E. "On Sylvia Plath." In *The Art of Sylvia Plath*, edited by Charles Newman, pp. 204–10. Bloomington: Indiana University Press, 1971.

Eliade, Mircea. *Myth and Reality*. New York: Harper & Row, 1963.

———. *Rites and Symbols of Initiation: The Mysteries of Birth and Rebirth*. New York: Harper & Row, 1968.

Fiedler, Leslie. *Love and Death in the American Novel*. New York: Stein & Day, 1966.

Friedrich, Otto. *Going Crazy*. New York: Simon & Schuster, 1976.

Graves, Robert. *The White Goddess: A Historical Grammar of Poetic Myth*. New York: Vintage Books, 1958.

Hardwick, Elizabeth. *Seduction and Betrayal: Woman and Literature*. New York: Random House, 1974.

Hardy, Barbara. "The Poetry of Sylvia Plath: Enlargement or Derangement?" In *The Survival of Poetry: A Contemporary Survey*, edited by Martin Dodsworth, pp. 164–92. London: Faber & Faber, 1970.

Holbrook, David. "R. D. Laing and the Death Circuit." *Encounter* 31, no. 2 (August 1968): 35–45.

———. "Sylvia Plath and the Problem of Violence in Art." *Cambridge Review* 90, no. 2187 (7 February 1969): 249–50.

———. *Sylvia Plath: The Poetry of Existence*. London: Athlone Press, 1976.

Homberger, Eric. "I am I." *Cambridge Review* 90, no. 2187 (7 February 1969): 251–52.

Howard, Richard. "Sylvia Plath." In *Alone with America*, pp. 413–21. New York: Atheneum, 1971.

Howe, Irving. "Sylvia Plath: A Partial Disagreement." *Harper's* 244 (January 1972): 88–92.

Hoyle, James. "Sylvia Plath: A Poetry of Suicidal Mania." *Literature and Psychology* 18 (1968): 187–203.

Hughes, Ted. "Notes on the Chronological Order of Sylvia Plath's Poems." In *The Art of Sylvia Plath*, edited by Charles Newman, pp. 187–95. Bloomington: Indiana University Press, 1971.

———. "Sylvia Plath's *Crossing the Water*: Some Reflections." *Critical Quarterly* 13, no. 2 (Summer 1971): 165–72.

Jones, A. R. "Necessity and Freedom: The Poetry of Robert Lowell, Sylvia Plath and Anne Sexton." *Critical Quarterly*, 7, no. 1 (Spring 1965): 11–30.

————. "On 'Daddy.'" In *The Art of Sylvia Plath*, edited by Charles Newman, pp. 230–36. Bloomington: Indiana University Press, 1971.

Kissick, Gary. "Plath: A Terrible Perfection." *Nation* 207 (16 September 1968); 245–47.

Kroll, Judith. *Chapters in a Mythology: The Poetry of Sylvia Plath*. New York: Harper & Row, 1976.

Lavers, Annette. "The World as Icon—On Sylvia Plath's Themes." In *The Art of Sylvia Plath*, edited by Charles Newman, pp. 100–135. Bloomington: Indiana University Press, 1971.

Levine, Philip. "Looking for an Opening." In *Naked Poetry*, edited by Stephen Berg and Robert Mezey, pp. 388–92. Indianapolis: Bobbs-Merrill, 1969.

Lowell, Robert. Foreword to *Ariel* by Sylvia Plath, pp. ix–xi. New York: Harper & Row, 1966.

————. *Life Studies*. New York: Random House, 1959.

Lucie-Smith, Edward. "Sea-imagery in the Work of Sylvia Plath." In *The Art of Sylvia Plath*, edited by Charles Newman, pp. 91–99. Bloomington: Indiana University Press, 1971.

Megna, Jerome Francis. "The Two-World Division in the Poetry of Sylvia Plath." Ph.D. dissertation, Ball State University, 1972.

Melander, Ingrid. "'The Disquieting Muses': A Note on a Poem by Sylvia Plath." *Research Studies of Washington State University* 39 (March 1971): 53–54.

————. *The Poetry of Sylvia Plath: A Study of Themes*. Gothenburg Studies in English, 25. Stockholm: Almqvist &.Wiksell, 1972.

Moraes, Dom. Review of *The Colossus*. *Time and Tide* 41, no. 46 (19 November 1960): 1413.

Morgan, Robin. *Monster*. New York: Vintage Books, 1972.

Newman, Charles. "Candor Is the Only Wile: The Art of Sylvia Plath." In *The Art of Sylvia Plath*, edited by Charles Newman, pp. 21–55. Bloomington: Indiana University Press, 1971.

————, ed. *The Art of Sylvia Plath: A Symposium*. Bloomington: Indiana University Press, 1971.

Nims, John Frederick. "The Poetry of Sylvia Plath—A Technical Analysis." In *The Art of Sylvia Plath*, edited by Charles Newman, pp. 146–52. Bloomington: Indiana University Press, 1971.

Oberg, Arthur K. "Sylvia Plath and the New Decadence." *Chicago Review* 20, no. 1 (March 1968): 66–73.

Oettle, Pamela. "Sylvia Plath's Last Poems." *Balcony*, no. 3 (1965): 47–50.

Ostriker, Alicia. "'Fact' as Style: The Americanization of Sylvia Plath." *Language and Society* 1 (1968): 201–12.

Paz, Octavio. *Conjunctions and Disjunctions*. New York: The Viking Press, 1969.

Perloff, Marjorie. "*Angst* and Animism in the Poetry of Sylvia Plath." *Journal of Modern Literature* 1, no. 1 (1970): 57–74.

_____. "'A Ritual for Being Born Twice': Sylvia Plath's *The Bell Jar*." *Contemporary Literature* 13, no. 4 (Autumn 1972): 507–22.

_____. "Extremist Poetry: Some Versions of the Sylvia Plath Myth." *Journal of Modern Literature* 2, no. 4 (November 1972): 581–88.

_____. *The Poetic Art of Robert Lowell*. Ithaca: Cornell University Press, 1973.

Plath, Sylvia. *Ariel*. New York: Harper & Row, 1966.

_____. BBC Interview with Peter Orr. In *The Poet Speaks*, edited by Peter Orr, pp. 168–74. London: Routledge & Kegan Paul, 1966.

_____. *The Bell Jar*. New York: Harper & Row, 1972.

_____. *The Colossus & Other Poems*. New York: Alfred A. Knopf, 1962.

_____. "The Cambridge Manuscript." *Cambridge Review* 90, no. 2187 (7 February 1969): 248–53.

_____. "Complaint of the Crazed Queen." *Times Literary Supplement* 68 (31 July 1969): 855.

_____. "Context." *London Magazine* 1 (1962): 45–46.

_____. *Crossing the Water*. New York: Harper & Row, 1971.

_____. *Crystal Gazer*. London: Rainbow Press, 1971.

_____. "Dialogue en Route." In *The Art of Sylvia Plath*, edited by Charles Newman, pp. 239–40. Bloomington: Indiana University Press, 1971.

_____. "Doomsday." *Harper's* 208 (May 1954): 29.

_____. "Dream with Clamdiggers." *Poetry* 89 (January 1959): 232–33.

_____. "Electra on Azalea Path." *Hudson Review* 13, no. 3 (Fall 1960): 415.

_____. "Go Get the Goodly Squab." *Harper's* 209 (November 1954): 47.

_____. "Initiation." *Seventeen* (January 1953), pp. 65, 92–94.

_____. "The Jailor." *Encounter* 22 (October 1963): 51.

_____. "Letter To a Purist." *Times Literary Supplement* 68 (31 July 1969): 855.

_____. *Lyonnesse*. London: Rainbow Press, 1971.

_____. "November Graveyard." *Mademoiselle* 62, no. 1 (November 1965): 134.

_____. "Ocean 1212-W." In *The Art of Sylvia Plath*, edited by Charles Newman pp. 266–72. Bloomington: Indiana University Press, 1971.

_____. "On the Decline of Oracles." *Poetry*, 94 (September 1959): 368–69.

_____. *Pursuit*. London: Rainbow Press, 1973.

_____. "Second Winter." *Lyric* 36, no. 1 (Winter 1956): 11.

_____. "The Snowman on the Moor." *Poetry* 90, no. 4 (July 1957): 229.

_____. "Stars over the Dordogne." *Poetry* 99 (March 1962): 346–47.

_____. "Temper of Time." *Nation* 181 (6 August 1955): 119.

_____. "To Eva Descending the Stair." *Harper's* 209 (September 1954): 63.

_____. "Two Lovers and a Beachcomber by the Real Sea." *Mademoiselle* 41 (August 1955): 52, 54.

_____. *Uncollected Poems*. London: Turret Books, 1965.

_____. *Winter Trees*. New York: Harper & Row, 1972.

Radin, Paul. *African Folktales and African Sculpture*. New York: Pantheon Books, 1952.

Ransom, John Crowe. *Selected Poems*. New York: Alfred A. Knopf, 1969.

Roethke, Theodore. *Collected Poems*. New York: Doubleday, 1966.

Rosenstein, Harriet. "Reconsidering Sylvia Plath." *Ms.* 1 (June 1973): 44–51, 96–99.

Rosenthal, M. L. "Metamorphoses of a Book." *Spectator* 218 (21 April 1967): 455–57.

_____. "Sylvia Plath." In *The New Poets*, pp. 79–89. New York: Oxford University Press, 1967.

Salamon, Lynda B. "'Double, Double': Perception in the Poetry of Sylvia Plath." *Spirit* 37, no. 2 (May 1970): 34–39.

Sexton, Anne. *All My Pretty Ones*. Boston: Houghton, Mifflin, 1961.

_____. "The Barfly Ought to Sing." In *The Art of Sylvia Plath*, edited by Charles Newman, pp. 174–81. Bloomington: Indiana University Press, 1971.

_____. *Live or Die*. Boston: Houghton, Mifflin, 1966.

Smith, Pamela. "The Unitive Urge in the Poetry of Sylvia Plath." *New England Quarterly* 45 (September 1972): 323–39.

Soby, James Thrall. *Giorgio de Chirico*. New York: Museum of Modern Art, 1955.

Spender, Stephen. "Warnings from the Grave." In *The Art of Sylvia*

Plath, edited by Charles Newman, pp. 199–203. Bloomington: Indiana University Press, 1971.

Stade, George. Introduction to *A Closer Look at Ariel: A Memory of Sylvia Plath* by Nancy Hunter Steiner. New York: Harper & Row, 1973.

Steiner, George. "Dying Is an Art." *Language and Silence: Essays on Language, Literature, and the Inhuman*, pp. 295–304. New York: Atheneum, 1970.

Steiner, Nancy Hunter. *A Closer Look at Ariel: A Memory of Sylvia Plath*. New York: Harper & Row, 1973.

Stevens, Wallace. *The Collected Poems of Wallace Stevens*. New York: Alfred A. Knopf, 1969.

Sumner, Nan McCowan. "Sylvia Plath." *Research Studies of Washington State University* 38 (June 1970): 112–21.

Thomas, Dylan. *The Collected Poems of Dylan Thomas*. New York: The New Directions Press, 1957.

Uroff, Margaret D. "Sylvia Plath and Confessional Poetry: A Reconsideration." *Iowa Review* 8, no. 1 (Winter 1977): 104–15.

———. "Sylvia Plath on Motherhood." *Midwest Quarterly* 15 (October 1973): 70–90.

Index

The Author

Jon Rosenblatt is assistant professor of English at Rhode Island College.

The Book

Typeface: Mergenthaler VIP Janson

Design and Composition: The University of North Carolina Press

Paper: Sixty-pound Olde Style by S. D. Warren Company

Binding cloth: Roxite B 53575 Linen by The Holliston Mills, Inc.

Printer and binder: Braun-Brumfield, Inc.

Published by The University of North Carolina Press